jennifer jill schwirzer

# i want it all

**ℝ**

REVIEW AND HERALD® PUBLISHING ASSOCIATION
HAGERSTOWN, MD 21740

The author assumes full responsibility for the accuracy of all facts and quotations as cited in this book.

This book was
Edited by Andy Nash
Copyedited by Lori Halvorsen and James Cavil
Designed by Trent Truman
Electronic makeup by Shirley M. Bolivar
Typeset: Cheltenham 11/14

PRINTED IN U.S.A.

06 05 04 03 02        5 4 3 2 1

**R&H Cataloging Service**
Schwirzer, Jennifer Jill, 1957-
    I want it all

    1. Teenagers—Prayer books and devotions—English.
2. Religious life.    I. Title.

                242.63

ISBN 0-8280-1628-3

# Dedication

To my daughters,
Kimberly Dawn and Alison Brook Schwirzer,
both teenagers.
Girl and Lollapooza, I love you! May you be forever with Jesus.

Also by this author:
*Testimony of a Seeker* (Pacific Press)
To order, call 1-800-765-6955.
Visit us at www.reviewandherald.com
for information on other Review and Herald products.

# Contents

# Introduction

So you want it all, do you? Well, you've come to the right place—a one-stop shop of lessons on how to get life's most important blessings. I should qualify that, though. You don't get them, because God already gave them. Yes, God "has blessed us with every spiritual blessing in the heavenly places in Christ, just as He chose us in Him before the foundation of the world, that we should be holy and blameless before Him in love" (Ephesians 1:3, 4). You don't get God's gifts; you receive them. And I hope this book will tell you just how to do that in a several ways:

*Obscure Bible Stories.* You've heard the awesome accounts of Moses, Gideon, and David from the time you were a little tyke, but have you heard about the crippled Mephibosheth, the Levite's concubine, or the timid Zipporah?

These stories let the unsung heroes of the Bible have their moment at the microphone. By the way, I took some liberties in telling the stories, filling in a detail here and there, but the basic story lines are from the Bible and the writings of Ellen White. Please don't consider the stories inspired in the same sense that the Word is inspired, but by all means let them inspire you to dig deeper into the Word!

*News and Views.* Here and there, I do the journalism thing— you know, taking some news item and drawing a spiritual lesson from it. What can we learn from star suicides and cross-dressing Olympic athletes? Read on and find out!

*Quirky parables.* When I ran out of true stories to tell, I made some up. This isn't fiction in the generic sense; it's allegory that sparks the imagination and draws forth a teaching.

*Cogitations.* "I think, therefore I am," someone has said. Certainly you didn't think I was just going to entertain you! You must legitimize your existence by cogitating (thinking) on the things that are shared.

*Try It Out.* I dare you to actually do the things I suggest in this devotional. Your life will never be the same, because you will have put the gospel into shoes—your shoes. Just sitting on your gluteus maximus won't really deepen your Christian walk; however, taking in the good news and then living the gospel will make you real.

So there you have it!

# Mary, Mother of Jesus

*"My soul magnifies the Lord, and my spirit has rejoiced in God my Savior. For He has regarded the lowly state of His maidservant; for behold, henceforth all generations will call me blessed. For He who is mighty has done great things for me, and holy is His name."*

LUKE 1:46-49, NKJV.

know what you're thinking. How can anyone say I'm a little-known Bible character when next to Jesus Himself, I'm probably the best known? Well, I have an answer for you, but I'll give you a hint first to see if you can guess. Here it is: There are two ways to remain unknown. The first is to do nothing exceptional; the second is to do something quite exceptional (such as giving birth to God's Son) but still remain a hostage to popular misconceptions. What I'm saying is that while I'm quite the subject of gossip, press exploitation, and media hype, very few really know me—the *real* me, that is.

Already some paintings have appeared depicting me as a gorgeous teenager holding a chubby baby. And the stable! In these pictures Baby Jesus is squeaky-clean on a bed of golden straw, equally squeaky, with a downy-white blanket such as only a queen could wrap her child in. Well, let me tell you a thing or two about giving birth in a stall. I think I can speak with authority on such matters.

First of all, there was no squeaky clean *anything*. Joseph and

# I Want It All

I had been traveling 70 miles, he walking and I on the back of a mule. Perhaps that's what made the baby come so soon—the bumpy riding, the wear and tear on my body when I should probably have stayed behind in Nazareth. When we finally found the vacant stall, I burst into tears as I thought of bearing any baby in that filthy place, much less the Messiah! Joseph held me until I could stand no more, and then I lay down in the filthy straw and among the beasts I bore their Maker. Oh, the flies! Flies in my eyes and nose, flies buzzing around our heads, even flies on my sweet Baby. I wrapped Him tight in the swaddling clothes with just His little face poking out.

Let me tell you about the swaddling clothes. They were not the ivory white blankets that privileged women wrap their infants in. No, this little Sovereign got wrapped in a burial shroud, which all travelers carry in case someone dies while in transit. Seeing Him bound up in the finery of death, I thought that perhaps this was God's way of saying that my little Son, *His* little Son, was born to die. Even in what was the happiest moment of my life, I felt the sword pierce my soul.

But that wasn't the first piercing sword I felt. Let me refer back to my poem at the top of the page. I patterned it after the poem of Hannah because she knew the same sense of dejection as I felt. She was childless—a terrible shame for a woman of Israel. I had a similar kind of shame.

The words "lowly state" are also called *tapeinosis,* which means "humiliation," or "abasement." It's the word we use today when we describe the crucifixion of our Lord and my Son. Amazing, God chose for His only Son a mother who tasted a bit of the same humiliation—*tapeinosis.* This shame is like the shame lepers feel when they are forced to wrench themselves from their family and live in quarantine. *Tapeinosis*—I knew it from the time I was young.

How did I know it? It would not be discreet of me to disclose the details, but suffice it to say that I was not a sought-after young woman. Oh, I know, the paintings! I am so beautiful in the paintings! Well, those are the paintings. I am not afraid to admit that I was, and am, on the homely side. Don't believe me? Consider this: My Son, whose sole human biological connection was to me, had "no form or comeliness . . . no beauty that we should desire Him" (Isaiah 53:2, NKJV). Who gave Him his non-beauty? God? Let me clarify: While Jesus was a beautiful person, He was not what we would call physically attractive.

Not that this was the great cause of His humiliation, for unattractiveness is no great setback for a man. A man can excel in scholastic and business matters, a man can overcome his home-liness with a powerful persona, but a woman . . . a woman must be beautiful to be accepted in our society. And I was not beautiful.

Every young Jewish girl had the same daydream. We would, we all hoped, grow up, get married, get pregnant, and give birth to the Messiah. Yes, I hoped against the odds that *I* would actu-ally be the one. But then as I grew into a plain, unnoticed young woman, my hope slipped away like sand from a broken hour-glass. As one by one my cohorts took the first step, then the sec-ond and the third, I became more and more tearfully aware that I wasn't even at step two—getting married. It wasn't because I was choosy when opportunities presented themselves—the op-portunities just plain didn't come. *Tapeinosis*.

But just when things seemed hopeless, when lines started to appear around my eyes like spider's webs on a stagnant tree branch, the opportunity to marry Joseph presented itself. Joseph, a man of sterling reputation, a man of honest industry. Joseph, a man with four sons! How could I think about the strain of bearing one of my own when he had the four little rascals and daughters besides? And they were rascals; I don't exaggerate. They picked on little Jesus without mercy and found all sorts of other mischief, as boys often do. Sometimes after a day of ex-hausting crowd control I was tempted to wonder what Joseph's first wife *really* died of . . .

I'm getting ahead of myself. I had been visited by the angel Gabriel, who brought all the desires and dreads of my heart in one paradoxical package. There was the joy of new motherhood pitted against the stigma of "illegitimate" childbearing. There was the pleasure of raising a perfect child contrasted with the pain of loving an outcast. Then there was the solemn privilege of knowing that my swaddling cloth held God incarnate conflicted with/objecting to/warring against the nearly unconscious hunch that my soft, cooing babe would grow into a man much taller and stronger than I and still find Himself fastened naked to a huge wooden post while all the godless universe laughed. *Tapeinosis.*

So this is the me you didn't know. The homely woman who knew rejection. The woman whose soul was pierced by the same sword of rejection as I saw Jesus hanging on a cross. The woman who fainted at the sight, only after crying, "My Son, my Son" over and over like a prophetic lamentation. If my mind had not been rendered incapable of clear thought by the sheer intensity of emotion, I might have been consoled in realizing that only one other Being in the universe could claim the same connection. "My Son, My Son," the Father must have cried, over and over, even as He hid His face from the sight. I hid my face too, I'm ashamed to say, crying into my hands until the tears ran down my wrists. My sorrow was more than the sorrow of a mother for her child. It was the sorrow of a disciple for a lost Messiah, and the loss of all that my people had hoped for . . . for 4,000 years and counting.

And perhaps you can imagine the corresponding joy I felt when my adoptive son John told me first that he had seen the graveclothes folded in the empty tomb. Sometime later Jesus met with us on Mount Olivet, an easy enough journey for my old bones to make. From this mountain He ascended; thinking of seeing Him again brings me overflowing joy.

And this is the beauty of *tapeinosis.* As deep as the roots of sorrow, just that high will ascend the branches of joy. I knew rejection, I knew humiliation, and I knew Jesus. Now I know His gospel as I never could have otherwise.

*(Get the story of Mary for yourself in Matthew 1:18-2:15; 27:55, 56;*
*Mark 15:40, 41; 16:1; Luke 1:46-58; 2:1-20; 24:10; Acts 1:1-14;*
*and* The Desire of Ages, *pages 44, 744, and 752.)*

## COGITATIONS

1. Do you think the mother of Jesus was beautiful? Why or why not?

2. How do humiliation and rejection prepare a person to experience joy?

3. We often judge by appearances. How can we avoid this trend, knowing that the true worth of a person often has nothing to do with the way they look?

4. Why do we care so much about how we look?

5. Think of someone you knew who was outwardly ugly but inwardly beautiful. What made you love that person?

6. Why do you think Jesus, who could have chosen any body He wanted, chose one that was not especially attractive? Would you have done the same thing?

# Human Barbie Doll

*"I have seen all the works that are done under the sun; and indeed, all is vanity and grasping for the wind."*

ECCLESIASTES 1:14, NKJV.

Cindy Jackson is listed in the *Guinness Book of World Records 2000* under the heading "Body Transformation." Cindy wins the prize for the person who has had the most plastic surgery—almost $100,000 worth ($99,600, to be exact). Cindy has had three full face-lifts, two nose operations, knee, abdomen, and jawline surgery, thigh liposuction, breast reduction *and* augmentation (make up your mind, Cindy!), and semipermanent makeup. Her look is based on Leonardo da Vinci's theory of a classically proportioned face, but she has been dubbed the "human Barbie doll" after a much more contemporary ideal of beauty. OK, so what does she actually look like?[1]

Well, only the face is shown in the *Guinness* book, but even the face (notice I don't say "her" face, because it's not!) isn't really that great. Pun intended, it's not all it was cracked up (cut up, sewed up, lasered up) to be. Oh, it's perfect, all right, not a flaw on it. She's my age, in her mid-40s, and if we each got a dollar per wrinkle, I would definitely come out on top. But there's something missing in this beautiful face. I think it's the brush strokes of the Creator. Now that it's possible to create one's own body, can people really come up with something as beautiful as God does when *He* makes a beautiful person? I have my doubts.

Sometimes I think it's unfair that not all men and women are created equally beautiful. We can't deny the fact that some people are born with prettier bone structures, skin textures, and hair types. Unfair or not, we can't despise beauty when God is the originator of it. At the same time, the world covets beauty as if it were the Holy Grail, the lost ark, and the winning lottery ticket all rolled into one. Where's the balance? Can we appreciate a beautiful face without worshiping it?

I think so, if we see in that beautiful face a reflection of the great Master Painter, then get to know the person as, well, a person. And the same thing goes for a homely person. Getting below the surface to the heart of an individual is like digging for gold. The gold-laden mountain may be lush and green or it may be barren and jagged, but what we really want is what's underneath, so we blast it open with dynamite regardless of how pretty or ugly it is. (No particular assumption should be made about the writer's commitment, or lack of commitment, to the cause of ecology.)

Henry James met the English novelist George Eliot (a woman) when she was 49 years old. He had developed an infatuation for her as a result of reading her famous novels. No doubt he had conjured up images of a mysterious beauty to accommodate his crush, but when he finally met her, he said, "She is magnificently ugly. . . . She has a low forehead, a dull gray eye, a vast pendulous nose, a huge mouth full of uneven teeth." But for Henry James, there was more than met the eye. "In this vast ugliness resides a most powerful beauty which, in a very few minutes, steals forth and charms the mind, so that you end as I ended, in falling in love with her."[2]

Do you see in Jesus someone who, although He had "no form or comeliness . . . no beauty that we should desire Him," could cause us to fall in love with Him if we got below the surface? He has gotten below our surface of sin, which is supremely ugly to Him, and seen our precious potential in Him. His love re-creates us in His beautiful image, and that's a beauty more than skin-deep.

## TRY IT OUT

Go through your house and count how many items you own that are designed to improve your appearance. This includes hairstyling products, makeup, hair removal paraphernalia, etc. (You will be amazed at the total count!) Then estimate the total dollar value of the items.

Think of someone in your life who has inner beauty. Tell that person you think so in a creative way, such as a note or card, an e-mail greeting card, or a handpicked bouquet.

Read the chapter "Calvary" in *The Desire of Ages* and draw a picture of what Jesus looked like after sleep deprivation, multiple beatings, two floggings, and the crown of thorns.

Find the hymn "O Sacred Head Now Wounded" and sing it a cappella while meditating on your picture.

## CROSS-EXAMINE THE WITNESS

 **Amber Heinrich from Roscoe, South Dakota, is a home-schooling senior. She loves to read and swim, but not at the same time.**

# I Want It All

QUESTION: AMBER, WHAT DO YOU THINK ABOUT THE ISSUE OF BEAUTY?

What thoughts do you associate with the word "lucky"? Mr. Webster defines it as "meeting with good luck; fortunate; auspicious." I guess I'm different—I see a magazine when I think of the word "lucky." I began receiving this publication a couple months ago because of some unused air miles. Lucky for me? Well . . . when the first issue landed in my mailbox I was enthralled—photos of beautifully dressed women, shopping secrets, catchy article titles, and dozens of beauty tips littered the cover. Hurriedly I flipped through the pages, finally settling on an article displaying the latest winter fashions. The styles shown promised to make me look like a million bucks—and indeed they should have, considering the amount on the price tags.

*No biggie,* I thought, going on to the beauty section. But as I studied the models' perfect faces, hair, and bodies, a realization hit me—no matter how much money I spent on clothes, or how much makeup I plastered on my face, nothing would ever make me as beautiful as the girls in the magazine. How *unlucky.*

A question popped into my head: *What does God think about all this? Does He even care about the way I dress or how my face looks?* Turns out He does! I discovered that in Matthew 6:28-30 Jesus tells us not to worry so much about what we should wear because He will clothe us. If He cares so much for the birds in the air, He will definitely take care of even my smallest need. An even better promise can be found in Philippians 3:21, where Paul tells us that when Jesus comes again He's going to change our imperfect bodies into new, beautiful ones! What a relief—what a promise! So the next time I feel discouraged about my lack of having the right clothes, perfect hair, and a pretty face, I'm going to remember that God loves me no matter what and He's looking forward to the day when I'll be His new creation. Isn't that lucky!

---

[1] *Guinness Book of World Records 2000* (Stamford, Conn.: Guinness World Records, Ltd., 2000), p. 151.

[2] Cathy Newman, "The Enigma of Beauty," *National Geographic,* January 2000, p. 104.

# Choice

# Pharaoh Neco

*"Your boasting is not good. Do you not know that a little leaven leavens the whole lump of dough?"*

1 Corinthians 5:6, NASB.

know you think I'm a heathen, and you're right. Idol worship, polygamy, spiritualism, decadence of all sorts—that's my lifestyle! And when you think Egyptian, you think "God's enemy," right? Yes, for the most part I have rejected the God of the Hebrews. But there was one instance He actually spoke to me. The ironic thing about it all is that I listened, and His own king did not. Go figure.

It was Josiah. I know, I know, the guy with the spotless reputation. The guy who instituted all the reforms and "raised high the standard," renouncing popular sin and calling the backsliders to their knees. Yes, he did a lot of good for Israel in bringing them back to their moral and spiritual roots, but as is often the case with people who receive praise for doing great things, he had a blind spot that proved his undoing. He was human! When a human being is used in any exercise of supernatural power, there's a tendency to become infatuated with the power itself. Josiah was used by the Hebrew God to facilitate a powerful national reform, but he got a little power hungry in the process—you know, prideful. At least that's my humble opinion.

Back up a little. In case you forgot the details of the story, Josiah was the son of Amon, a real fascist of a guy, who probably inherited that character trait from his *own* father, who was the bloodiest king Israel has ever known—the tyrant Manasseh. With all this despotism and idolatry in Josiah's past, it was truly remarkable that he chose to dedicate his life to the God of Judah, but he did just that. I admire and respect him for it.

Ascending the throne at 8 years of age, he sparked the people with hope that the nation might not continue its downward course into the muck of idol worship and sin. The people's hope was not in vain. The high priest discovered the lost books of the law, which Josiah then read in the hearing of all the people, calling them to massive reform. And he acted on his words. He exterminated all the false prophets, even digging up the bones of the same from centuries before and burning them upon the altar. He decimated the shrines left over from Solomon's idolatrous wives and held a Passover for the first time in centuries. He scoured the land for idols and tossed, burned, or destroyed them all. And all this while he was in his 20s!

About 10 years after the great reform, though, he died tragically. The saddest note in his eulogy was the undeniable fact that he had brought this unnecessary death upon himself. It was the untimely death of a good man, and I say that as—technically speaking—an enemy.

I had come to make war with the city of Carchemish. I was helping the Assyrians to fight Babylon, which was threatening to take over the whole world. I was indirectly protecting Judah, but Josiah didn't see it that way. At 39 he was still feeling pretty macho, and he came charging up to the scene of battle, saying that he wanted to take me on. Don't ask me why. For such a deliberative, practical guy this move seemed out of character. Chalk it up to male hormones getting the better of him. Or maybe an early midlife crisis.

I sent messengers to tell him to back off. "What contention do we have with each other?" I said. "We're at peace, King of Judah! I'm not going to war with *you,* but with Babylon. Your God wants me to fight them! So stop interfering with God, whom you have served all your life! God is with me, Josiah, and if you fight me, God will destroy *you!*" I felt really strange preaching to a holy man, but the situation called for it.

He didn't listen. Ever the assertive, decisive type, Josiah made a choice that proved fatal. As was the common practice, he disguised himself and ran headlong into the fracas. I'm sorry to tell you that he was shot through by my highly skilled archers on the plain of Megiddo. He cried to his servants that he was wounded, and they took him to Jerusalem, but he died a short time later from internal injuries and blood loss.

What can be said about the demise of a good man, especially when that demise came as a result of a good man making a bad choice? More than anyone ever had, Josiah convinced me of the power of his God. The irony of it all is that he also convinced me of the frailty of humanity. Furthermore, that frailty is at its greatest when people try to make themselves powerful. Even a great man of God was not beyond making such a blunder.

All Judah and Jerusalem mourned for him. The prophet Jeremiah lamented for him. To this day the singers recall Josiah in their sad songs. I miss the guy! But we all can take a couple lessons away from the experience. One, don't reject God's message if it comes through someone you consider an outsider. God is the God of all flesh, including Egyptian flesh. All it took for me to go from "outsider" to "insider" was believing Him. Two, don't let power go to your head. Sure, make your conquests for God, but don't attribute your victories to yourself. If you do, you might wind up discovering just how weak you really are. Hopefully you will realize this without having to get shot through with one of my arrows.

*"Humble yourselves, therefore, under the mighty hand of God, that He may exalt you at the proper time, casting all your anxiety upon Him, because He cares for you. Be of sober spirit, be on the alert. Your adversary, the devil, prowls about like a roaring lion, seeking someone to devour."*

1 Peter 5:6-8, NASB.

*(Get the story of Pharaoh Neco for yourself in 2 Kings 23:21-33; 2 Chronicles 35:20-27;* Prophets and Kings, *pages 381-406.)*

## COGITATIONS

1. Why does the Bible record the sins of good people?

2. What are the problems with black-and-white thinking, in which the good guys are always good and the bad guys are always bad?

3. Was Josiah a legalist because he carried out reforms in Judah?

4. What does Josiah's behavior in the battle with Pharaoh Neco indicate about his character?

# The Power of a Single Choice

t's 7:00 a.m., and the new shift comes into the emergency room. Immediately an alarm sounds, and news comes of two teen victims of an auto accident. They were headed for home two hours away when their truck flipped off a bridge. The boy looks bad, but the girl not so bad. She's alert and she can move her arms and legs, but she says her neck is sore. She's waiting for X-rays.

The doctor calls her parents, one of the hardest jobs in the ER. She lets them know about the wreck, that their daughter looks pretty good but that she's had no X-rays. The parents are on their way.

Neck X-rays are completed first. Her head is immobilized in cervical restraints, which come off when the neck X-rays come back negative. The doctor finds a fractured knee and shoulder.

"My neck is still hurting," she says. There are none of the classic signs of neck fracture, such as numbness, tingling, loss of movement, but the doctor is struggling with a voice in her head.

The doctor ignores the voice and chalks the pain up to whiplash. Life goes on in the ER, until a few minutes later the girl says her hands are tingling. Immediately the doctor again immobilizes her neck, berating herself silently for not listening to the voice that spoke moments before. Now she chooses to respond to the voice, hoping it's not too late. The films go back to X-ray with the urgent request to take a second look. The report comes back; there is a break in her second cervical vertebra. Nerves to her entire body pass through this bone—nerves that control breathing, movement, feeling.

Inside, the doctor is screaming. Outside, she is calm.

Once the head is immobilized, sensation returns to the girl's hands. Mother and father arrive. "Your daughter is alive," the doctor says, "but her neck is broken. She's not paralyzed, but she will have to wear a brace that screws into her head for the next few months."

The doctor wheels the girl to her hospital room, where a neurosurgeon places the head screws. The girl is brave and grateful. She thanks the doctor for caring so well for her.

Later the doctor receives flowers from the girl with a note promising to stay in touch.

The doctor doesn't sleep well that night, knowing what might have been.*

---

* Adapted from Mark Brown, *Emergency! True Stories From the Nation's ERs* (New York: Villard Books, 1996), pp. 93, 94.

# The Sockless Scientist

lbert Einstein never wore socks, calling them a waste of time. This gave him time to think about more important things, such as the theory of relativity he is famous for. By far the most renowned scientist of the twentieth century, Einstein made his mark in the world by conceiving of a formula that proved that things got heavier when they moved faster, and that time slowed down at high speeds. According to his calculations, if you took a trip at the speed of light you would come back younger than your twin sister.

The discovery of $E = mc^2$ was all well and good until years later when Einstein saw his theory used to create a monster that would destroy countless lives. His story in some ways resembles the story of Adam, who made a choice that had a devastating effect upon every one of us. "Just as through one man sin entered into the world, and death through sin, and so death spread to all men, because all sinned" (Romans 5:12, NASB). Adam didn't realize what long-term ramifications his actions would have, and neither did Mr. Einstein.

Albert was never a very good student. He couldn't even speak fluently until he was 9, and some teachers considered him backward. Those around him couldn't see the wheels of his mind churning, or they would have thought differently. While he failed classes in grammar, he was pondering deep scientific concepts that were far beyond his years.

He tried to enroll in the Federal Institute of Technology in Switzerland for college courses, but failed the entrance exam. Finally entering another school, he began to contemplate the deep questions of physics that were coming upon the world's scientific community. He graduated from school and found a job as a low-grade clerk at a patent office, but he was living on another plane, the plane of scientific theory, while he fulfilled his daily duties.

It was in 1905 that the sockless wonder published his first memoirs on the theory of relativity. This began the slow process of making Albert Einstein a household name. He used his growing influence to denounce World War I, which broke out in 1914, writing a manifesto for peace and international cooperation. As his fame grew, he increasingly manifested opposition to war and a commitment to world peace. Then World War II began to brew.

In 1933 Adolf Hitler's Nazi party came into power, and with it anti-Jewish hysteria. Because he was Jewish, anti-Nazi, pacifist, and scientifically astute, Einstein's books were banned and publicly burned. His portrait was published on the first page of a book of national "enemies" and underneath it was the caption "Not yet hanged."

Perhaps the most remarkable thing about Einstein's life is that the great discovery of a pacifist led to the development of the atom bomb. In 1939 Einstein wrote a letter to President Roosevelt telling him of the possibility of this new type of bomb, and warning of the danger that the Nazis might develop it first. Several years later he sent another letter to the president, pleading with him not to use the atom bomb, which the U.S. had developed since the first letter. In spite of his attempt to stop it, the first atom bomb was dropped by the U.S. on the city of Hiroshima in Japan. About 100,000 people were killed instantly, and many more died of the aftereffects.*

For his remaining years, Einstein called for the abolition of nuclear weapons. "Science has brought forth this danger," he said, "but the real problem is in the hearts and minds of men."

Adam would have to agree with that. Because of the sin that has invaded our planet like a nuclear fallout, we are all condemned to death apart from God's mercy. Now our hearts and minds are prone to destroy others and even God Himself. Fortunately, there is a Second Adam, who has reversed the sentence of condemnation brought upon us by the first Adam. The bomb of sin was detonated in Him while He hung on the cross of Calvary, shattering His soul in a mushroom cloud of condemnation. Because He took the heat for us, we can escape the effects of Adam's choice.

This is the cost of freedom. God would settle for nothing less than intelligent, loving worship, and so He allowed humans to choose. Humans chose to sin, but God still wasn't finished. He gave His only Son so that we could have a second chance, a second choice. Whatever you do, don't despise the Gift.

*"So then as through one transgression there resulted condemnation to all men, even so through one act of righteousness there resulted justification of life to all men."*

ROMANS 5:18, NASB.

## TRY IT OUT

Write a one-page essay titled "The Cost of Freedom." To remind yourself of the thinking of our forebears, and how highly they valued free choice, read the United States Constitution. You can get a copy at: http://www.nara.gov/exhall/charters/constitution/constitution.html>

## CROSS-EXAMINE THE WITNESS

 *Our witness, Alison Schwirzer, is a student at South Lancaster Academy in Massachusetts. Alison loves to sing and aspires to become a physician. A singing doctor, anyone?*

QUESTION: GOD TOOK A HUGE RISK IN GIVING US FREEDOM OF CHOICE. WHY?

It all started when Adam and Eve sinned. Everything was perfect, including the fact that God gave them free choice. He took a huge risk in doing this. As you know, the snake tempted them, and they were stupid enough to do what it suggested—eat the fruit. This caused them to be thrown out of the garden. They didn't have very good lives after that. And now we, the descendants of Adam and Eve, also have tough lives. (I'm sure you know what I mean.)

Now here we are making our own choices from day to day. And a lot of them are really stupid. And because God let us have freedom of choice, He sacrificed the only child He had to save a race of people who put Him through a lot of emotional pain. Was this worth it for Him?

To answer that question, ask another. Why did God give us freedom of choice? It's a simple answer: God did not want to make a race that loved Him because they *had* to. He didn't want to make a race of robots. I'm glad of that! He wanted us to love Him because of our *choice*. He really loves us a lot to take such a risk.

---

* Nigel Hunter, *Einstein* (New York: Bookwright Press, 1987).

# Equality

# Zipporah

*"But now in Christ Jesus you who formerly were far off have been brought near by the blood of Christ. For He Himself is our peace, who made both groups into one, and broke down the barrier of the dividing wall."*

EPHESIANS 2:13, 14, NASB.

*"And He has made from one blood every nation of men to dwell on all the face of the earth."*

ACTS 17:26, NKJV.

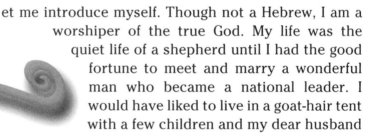

et me introduce myself. Though not a Hebrew, I am a worshiper of the true God. My life was the quiet life of a shepherd until I had the good fortune to meet and marry a wonderful man who became a national leader. I would have liked to live in a goat-hair tent with a few children and my dear husband as companions. There was nothing I wanted more than to be the wife of an honest, hardworking man. The wife of a head of state? I never imagined it in my wildest dreams, and I *never* dreamed it would be a foreign state. I am Ethiopian, and Moses is the leader of Israel. You can pick me out in a crowd, because my skin is several shades darker than the rest. I suppose you would say I'm a member of a minority.

People love to criticize, which is what is so hard about public life. They criticize words I speak or don't speak, the way I raise my children, the way I treat Moses, and of course the color of my skin. My skin color doesn't matter to Moses; in fact, he loves my skin, calling it beautiful, especially compared to the pale faces of the Egyptian women who never work a moment in the sun. I feel beautiful around him and ugly around the critics. Nothing about me changes, only the lens through which I see myself.

You should hear the story of how I met this wonderful man. My six sisters and I were at the well one day to draw water for Father's flocks. The shepherds of the area were quite an ornery bunch, and they were trying to prevent us from drawing, when to our surprise an Egyptian man sitting by the well stood up and began to shout, "Leave them alone, and let them draw!"

The faces of the shepherds registered shock: *Why does this Egyptian care to defend a bunch of shepherd girls?* Scrutinizing him, they backed away, finally leaving the well to us. Then this foreigner with the shaved face and linen tunic took one of our goatskin pouches and began to draw water, emptying it into the troughs. The flocks drank while the girls and I shyly inspected our hero. Although it was a custom to exercise hospitality to strangers, we were all too shy. Glancing at him one last time from under our head coverings, we started for home.

"Why are you home so early?" our father, Jethro, asked. Our seven voices wove in and out of each other in excitement:

"An Egyptian." "He chased the shepherds away!" "He helped us draw water!" "I think he's cute!" *Giggle, giggle.*

"Why didn't you invite him home? Go find him and bring him back for supper!" our bighearted father said.

I was the oldest, so the natural choice of a messenger. I admit I was scared and thrilled at the same time. I ran and walked back to the well, running because of eagerness to see the Egyptian, walking when I thought of how I wanted to appear composed and mature. As the well began to focus in my vision, I could see him through the heat waves. Slowing to a walk, I tried to look a little bored. He looked up when I drew near, and seemed to recognize me. Now shyness froze my tongue for

**27**

about the time it takes to walk 10 whole steps, and when I finally could speak, my voice was a whisper, as if I was trying to scream while dreaming.

"I—I am one of the shepherd girls you helped. Father—*my* father—would like you to come home with me—*us*—and stay as my—*our*—guest," I said.

He seemed amused and kind at the same time—aware of my foibles, accepting me anyway. I loved him already.

And so it was that the good-looking Egyptian came to our home. This was an exciting event for us girls, although we tried hard to refrain from the usual giggling and chatter. While most of the man's verbal communication was with Father, he felt our presence, and we felt his in the way that is typical of young men and women. I would watch him carefully until he would feel my eyes upon him. Then he would cast a glance in my direction, which would send my eyes somewhere else—the tent door, my lap, the other girls. Each time this little game was played there was a fleeting moment of eye contact that put a flutter in my stomach as if I were riding a camel downhill. Because of this sub-liminal-type communication, we knew each other well by the time our first night together rolled around. Oh, did I shock you? Don't worry; we were married.

Gradually I learned the secrets of his life; he was not an Egyptian, but an Egyptian-bred Hebrew, who at one time had a special calling from God to free all the thousands of Hebrew slaves in bondage to Pharaoh. He was running from a murder charge and wondering how he would ever appear before Pharaoh again, wondering if God still wanted to use him, wondering if he would ever amount to much. In a sense he was a broken man, a once-powerful prince turned lowly shepherd plagued with doubts and fears. I loved him all the more for his neediness.

Then one day He encountered God in a burning bush. You know the story. He was to return to Egypt and tell Pharaoh to re-lease about 2 million of his slaves. I tried to be brave when we parted, but I admit that as his silhouette was swallowed up by the desert horizon, I collapsed in grief.

News finally came that Moses and the Exodus had been a success, that Pharaoh and his troops were swallowed in the Red Sea. The Hebrews were an unruly bunch, prone to outbreaks of murmuring, but Moses was courageous and had hopes of entering the Promised Land in a few months. We traveled to meet Moses where he was camped with his people.

The pace of our lives was insane after that, one big event following another. First, the Ten Commandments; then the golden calf and the appointment of the 70 elders when the people grumbled. Soon after came the quail and the plague that broke out when the people gorged themselves. Timid as I was, there were times when I felt like running into the center of the camp and screaming, "Will you people *grow up?*"

Just after the quail incident came the heartache of my life. It was from Miriam, Moses' sister. Yes, the Miriam who bravely watched Baby Moses as his basket bobbed in the Nile, the Miriam who then shrewdly bargained with Pharaoh's daughter so that Jochebed could not only nurse her baby, but get paid for it. This vivacious Miriam had led all of Israel in a dance of victory on the shores of the Red Sea and taught them countless songs she had written herself. I've never known a more creative, talented person. Unfortunately, she was a racist.

Envy was the weak spot in her character. Both she and Aaron had felt left out of the high-level leadership decisions for some time. Miriam blamed this on me, but the truth was that she resented me because I was a Midianite. She was never happy about our marriage, feeling that Moses should have chosen a Hebrew wife. She claimed that national pride was necessary to maintain the morale of the people. Oh, but the fact is that pride and prejudice are twin sisters. Pride is a pinnacle from which we look down on everyone beneath us. I could see it in her eyes the first time she looked into my darker-than-hers face.

"Oh. You are the wife my brother has chosen . . . well, hello." So cool, so contained, she was like one of the Egyptian cucumbers the Israelites lusted for in the wilderness. This coldness soon waxed into criticism that stung like a nettle. It was so hard to be resented by a woman everyone loved! Days, weeks, months passed in silent suffering. Her prejudice toward me grew in proportion to her envy of Moses, until that envy finally boiled over and Miriam's sin was seen by everyone. This was the turning point. Until then, I endured the loneliness of a stranger in a strange land. This is how it all happened:

"Has the Lord spoken only through Moses? Hasn't He spoken through us as well?" Miriam and Aaron shouted while Moses stood in silence.

Suddenly a deep rumbling was heard, like ocean waves somehow forming words. It was God's voice. Bold, red-faced Miriam grew pale when she heard the sound. Again the ocean voice:

"You three come out to the tent of meeting!"

Events followed in rapid succession. The three siblings went obediently, tremblingly, to the tent. A pillar of cloud appeared at the doorway. Miriam and Aaron were called. More words came forth from the mouth of the Lord, and when the cloud was finally withdrawn, Miriam was covered over with the white death of leprosy. Aaron began to beg Moses to help, and my meek, gentle husband, who easily could have left her to die, wretched out a prayer in her behalf.

Miriam was healed, but not without a little lesson from God, a lesson she has not forgotten. She was to be shut up outside the camp for seven days, as any cleansed leper would have to be. This was a great humiliation for two reasons: her high-profile position, and the fact that the entire camp had to halt their journey while she waited out her sentence.

Things were better after that. Miriam began to treat me with increasing civility, until today we are closest friends. I was one of those fortunate ones who watched God deal directly with someone whose prejudices brought me pain and heartache. I know, however, that there are millions who never see the wrong of racial prejudice righted in their lifetimes. Ethnic wars, gangs, religious oppression, discrimination, and segregation bring bruises to bodies and minds everywhere on this fractured planet. But isn't it ironic that the racism that mounts into bloodshed actually reveals our sameness? Think about it. A man with one color skin attacks a man with another color skin, opening that skin to reveal what lies beneath it, and whether the skin is black, brown, white, or something in between, the blood is always the same bright, universal red.

*(Get the story of Miriam for yourself in Exodus 2:15-25; 4:24-26; Numbers 12; and* Patriarchs and Prophets, *pages 247, 300, and 383, 384.)*

## COGITATIONS

1. Did Zipporah respond correctly to Miriam's prejudice? Is it good to be passive when someone tries to harm us? If not, what action should be taken?

2. How does racial prejudice lead to more racial prejudice?

3. Should jobs ever be denied a person because of skin color? If so, when? Should jobs ever be denied a person because of sexual preference? If so, when? Are these two issues different? How?

4. Have you ever been the object of prejudice? How has God enabled you to process the experience, if at all? Would you call it a blessing in disguise? Why or why not?

# Forget the Alamo!

*"Forgive us our debts, as we also have forgiven our debtors."*

MATTHEW 6:12, NASB.

*"And be kind to one another, tender-hearted, forgiving each other, just as God in Christ also has forgiven you."*

EPHESIANS 4:32, NASB.

aybe "Forgive the Alamo!" is a better way to say it. We can forgive hurt, even hurt that's *impossible* to forget.

The Alamo is a fort in Texas where 183 Americans, including Davy Crockett, fought against 3,000 Mexican soldiers. Every American was killed. Mexico owned Texas at the time, but the American settlers cried, "Remember the Alamo!" as a way to unite people against Mexico. Eventually the U.S. bought southwestern Texas, although some Mexicans still believe it was stolen.

Believe it or not, this 1836 battle lies at the foundation of the Hispanic gang wars now present in almost every U.S. city. In a nutshell, the tensions between Mexicans and Americans, which began at the Alamo, continued. Many of the poor Mexicans, or "Chicanos," ended up in inner-city Los Angeles, where they felt divided from American society. They were poor and largely uneducated. Poor people often feel powerless, and in their alienation from society they band together to try to gain the power they feel they need.

African-American gangs, the Crips and the Bloods, had their beginning in the violent crimes committed against Blacks around the 1950s, and in zoning laws that excluded Blacks from certain neighborhoods in Los Angeles. Black Americans were not permitted in most suburbs, which forced them to live in the ghettos. Again, powerless people formed "ethnically isolated subsocieties" in an effort to acquire power they couldn't gain in the society at large. In the 1960s a teen gang called the Cribs, a name that refers to their youth, was formed. This gang closely mimicked the look of Black Panthers, radical Black activists of the fifties and sixties. Not only did the Cribs wear black leather jackets; they carried canes. When a group of Cribs attacked several old ladies, the ladies referred to them as "cripples" because of the canes, and so Cribs became Crips. Because the Crips were so dominant, several other African-American gangs united to form the Bloods in an effort to challenge them and limit their power. What began as one color joining with another color to fight (interracial fighting) ended in the same color fighting against itself (intraracial fighting).*

There are Asian gangs, Irish gangs, Italian gangs, and motorcycle gangs. There are "hybrid gangs" that cross territorial borders and spread themselves over many cities. There are gangs that don't call themselves gangs, but cliques, crews, or posses. Gangs are essentially little junior mafias—remember, a member of the Mafia is called a *"gangster."* Al Capone, known as Scarface, had his beginning in the Five Points Gang in New York City and went on to become one of the most widely known and feared Mafia leaders of all time. The gangs sometimes confess their criminal character in their names: Devil's Disciples, Hell's Angels, Black Gangster Disciples, etc.

You get the picture. Poverty and alienation from the society force ethnic groups into the inner cities. There they band together to try to achieve through crime what they can't get any other way—a feeling of belonging, of power. Once they taste a little power, they want a lot more. As the gangs grow, fracturing begins, until interracial violence becomes intraracial violence. Where does it end?

It ends with forgiveness. No, we can't *forget* our history, but we can forgive the wrong done to us as individuals and as an ethnic group. God adopted the entire human race in Christ, and so in essence we are one family. If we accept our position in Him, Jesus will give us a new outlook in which our enemies become our blood relations. Through faith, we are able to live free of bitterness and hate (see the above scriptures), but without God's power in our lives, we will only add to the problem.

## TRY IT OUT

1. You can't change the color of your skin, but you can change your appearance. Dress like a street person: scruffy clothes, disheveled hair, maybe a blackened tooth or two. Go about your business and see the difference in the way people treat you. If you're really brave, attend a church where you don't know anyone.

2. There are cliques in every school based on such things as ethnicity, social strata, and popularity. Make a friend from another clique, or from no clique at all, and get to know that person's heart.

3. Has someone hurt you? Perhaps you have avoided them, but the bitterness is still there. Try going on your knees before God and claiming His power to forgive. Then go to the person with a loving, forgiving attitude, acting upon your prayer. See if they respond. If they do, you may eventually be able to tell them how they hurt you. Surprisingly, these types of rocky-beginning friendships can be the deepest and most long-lasting.

## CROSS-EXAMINE THE WITNESS

 *Our witness is Taryn Honey from Mount Pearl, Newfoundland, Canada. She is originally from Cape Town, South Africa. One of Taryn's favorite activities is laughter, but when addressing the question of racism, she gets very serious.*

QUESTION: WHAT CAN ONE PERSON DO TO DISSOLVE RACIAL TENSION AND CLASS PREJUDICE?

I think that one person can do much to counteract the racial tension and class prejudice that so many classroom atmospheres contain. Probably one of the easiest ways is for you yourself to be open-minded to those around you. Look at people from the inside out instead of the usual scrutinizing of outward appearance. Don't be quick to judge others based on who the class thinks is popular. Who actually decides which people are cool and which not? You yourself need to decide which people are cool to you; don't worry about what others think. Hey—God thinks we're all cool! The Bible tells us that we need to love one another as we would want to be loved. Go talk to someone whom people think is "out of your social circle." See how much fun other people can be and what new things you can learn about your fellow classmates. You may just make a good friend and have the time of your life! And when other people see how much fun you are having with your new friends, they might soon follow.

---

* Nagia Web site: www.nagia.org/Crips_and_Bloods.htm.

# Naboth

*"Indeed, all who desire to live godly in Christ Jesus will be persecuted."*

2 TIMOTHY 3:12, NASB.

y dear family,

I am awaiting trial here in Samaria . . . town square. Things do not look good at all. I have a few moments while the people assemble to write down these thoughts. I want all of you to know the truth: You mean everything to me. I'm not afraid of dying, but I am a little afraid of leaving you to live without me.

A fast has been proclaimed, and the elders and nobles (if you can call them noble) are gathering. Two stand-ins have been hired by Jezebel to testify against me in what will be vintage Jezebelian jurisprudence—an insult to the concept of justice. I can't wait to hear the wild story these scarecrows come up with. I wonder what their accusation will be.

The truth is, I am guilty of the high crime of loving you more than life itself.

Here is the story in nutshell form (nutshell is all I have time for):

As you know, Ahab wanted to buy the vineyard from me. This plot has been in our family for years before the palace was even built. Ahab wanted to rip out the vines and put in a vegetable garden so he could have his kitchen supplies right near the palace. He offered me a pretty shekel for it—saying he would give me either a better vineyard or money. I won't deny that this tempted me for a moment, but the levitical law kept ringing in my ears: "No inheritance of the sons of Israel shall be transferred from tribe to tribe" (Numbers 36:7, NASB). The plot was to stay in the family, to be passed on as an heirloom. In making this law, God made it possible for fathers to know their families were taken care of, even after their decease. It looks now as if you might lose me and the land at the same time, but the God who made a law to protect families will find some other way to care for you.

When I turned down the option to sell, Ahab had one of his toddler fits. He flopped onto his bed and stuck out his lower lip, refusing to eat. I would never describe what Jezebel and Ahab have between them as love, but they do have a certain dysfunctional collaboration. The codependent queen came to her pouting king and asked, "What's the matter, baby?"

He gave her his sob story.

At that moment the first lady turned into the dragon lady. Insulted on Ahab's behalf, she promised to get him the vineyard. Really, I think she loves to play the role of avenger and waits for chances like these. She wrote letters in the king's name and sealed them with his seal. This event actually exemplified the dynamics of their political teamwork—Jezzy is the brains behind the operation; Ahab is a puppet.

What the letters contained was a scheme to hire two conscienceless pawns to lie about me. As I said, I am waiting to hear the story they will make up. My moments left are few, but I had to let you know that what brought me to the stoning pit was crime not on my part, but on theirs. I did what I did out of love for you, my family, and my God.

They are calling court into session. I must close now. If I live, I will throw this letter away and tell you the story myself. If I die, this will get to you. I hope you never read these words, but if you do, let them be proof of my love.

I am yours,
Naboth

*(Get the story of Naboth for yourself in 1 Kings 21*
*and* Prophets and Kings, *pages 205, 206.)*

## COGITATIONS

1. Naboth's family was the most important "institution" to him, ranking higher than his country. Does this reflect God's view of the importance of the family?
2. The family is the building block of society. What happens to societies in which the family loses importance?

# A Matter of Love or Death

*"Now abide faith, hope, love, these three; but the greatest of these is love."*

1 CORINTHIANS 13:13, NKJV.

*"We know that we have passed out of death into life, because we love the brethren. He who does not love abides in death."*

1 JOHN 3:14, NASB.

 t is widely believed that four things are necessary for survival: air, food, water, and shelter. Some would add clothing, but the nudists would disagree with that. I would like to add one more: love. It is my belief that we need *love* in order to survive.

No, not a date on Saturday night; not a clique of friends that agree with our taste in clothing. Real, warm, assuring affection. True, honest acceptance. We can't live without it.

More specifically, babies need to know that they are loved in order to develop properly. An orphanage in South America had 97 orphans. Seventy-six of them died over a few years time for no apparent reason. It was finally discovered that the infants had developed a rare disease called Marasmus, which means literally "wasting away." Why did the babies start wasting away? Because they weren't being held. They had good nutrition, clean surroundings, and warm clothes, but they had no cuddling and holding as most babies have. Without the skin-to-skin contact, the babies developed a hunger, a skin hunger, which was never satisfied. They died of starvation—skin-contact starvation. Since then much study has been done on orphans. Another group of orphans was found to have "dead" areas of their brains because of lack of skin stimulation in infancy. One thing is for sure—babies are born for love.

Maybe this picture is a bit hopeless-looking to you. Maybe you know someone, or you yourself *are* someone, who didn't get the affection you needed as an infant. Don't despair. The God who raised the dead can resurrect your brain tissue and heal the damage that imperfect parenting caused. Now look at it in the positive: God created the family as the second "womb," a place where children can grow and develop in the environment of love. Since the devil knows that a loving home environment will foster intelligent, sensitive people, he focuses his diabolical designs upon ruining the family. If you are living in a family he has shattered, take courage—by God's grace the downward spiral can end with your generation. *You* can invite Jesus into the midst of your own home, and in so doing build a house on the rock that will withstand stress from within and without.

# The Report

have called this gathering of staff members to announce the results of our study of the effects of the electronic eye, which was created about 50 years ago. This study is very broad-based and exhaustive, and the language is quite technical, so I invite you to read carefully the report you have in your hands in your leisure time, if you have any. I will be capsulizing the study today so that you might be encouraged that this device is having the result that we hoped it would have.

"As you know, we cannot take full credit for the invention of the electronic eye. Our enemy gave information to scientists years ago, hoping to see a device created that would make it possible for him to convey his propaganda to millions of people at a time. Since we have a more widespread influence upon the people of the planet, though, we have been able to use this creation for our own purposes. Call it the hijacking of an invention if you like. Look on your report, page 345, table 37, and you will see a bar-graph comparison of our programming, neutral programming, and enemy programming. As you can see, the enemy's programming is minimal compared to ours in both number of hours and number of viewers. We are far more popular. I hope you feel satisfied knowing this.

"The effects of our invention are detailed in the last section of your report, starting with page 859. As you will see in the section outline, there are three main effects we have been able to document. First, the addictive effect upon the brain of the individual who becomes a slave to our programming. Second, the effect upon the morals of the society at large. While these effects are important and crucial to our plan of ruination, the third effect is the one I wish to dwell upon the most heavily—the effect of our programming upon *relationships*.

"As you know, I hate the narrowness of the nuclear family. I have striven to broaden the concept of the family to include just about any combination of people living in one habitation, with or without long-term commitment. We want people to see the father/mother/children arrangement as antiquated and destructive to free thought and creative development. I have sought to break down this structure through two primary methods. First, permanent legal separation through divorce of parents. This method has succeeded in about 50 percent of the cases. For those resistant to this method, who because of societal or religious constraints are determined not to break the marriage contract, I use my second method. This involves divorce of a more subtle emotional and psychological nature. I lead the family members into complete communication breakdown so that they become strangers to one another even though they remain legally bound and living under one roof.

"This is where our device comes in. Our creation is fast becoming a constant in every home. Even some of the poorest shack-dwellers can afford one of our devices, as they are so massproduced that market competition drives their prices down. I am so delighted with these results that I have elected to reward all of us with a post-conference party . . . yes, yes, I knew you would be pleased with that. I have arranged for sumptuous food and expensive entertainment—several well-known rock bands and comedians. Now, if you will please quiet down, I will finish.

"I want to summarize the effect of our device upon family relationships. When messages, the majority of which are inspired by my own genius, come pouring into the home for most of the waking hours of the day, two results are seen. One, the messages themselves program the mind toward selfishness, disrespect, animosity, rage, and rebellion. These things thwart the better impulses of love and community, which foster the well-being of the family. Two, communication breakdown results. The watchers become accustomed to passive stimulation, one-way communication, and eventually lose the ability to engage in conversation with one another. The device essentially brings those who use it into a pseudo reality, eventually unfitting them to deal with reality itself. The result is the fracturing of family relationships. Hooray!

# I Want It All

"I have briefly summarized the results of just one aspect of the report, an aspect most encouraging to me. Exciting, isn't it? Now, bring on the booze, the food, the dancers. Hang on to those reports; I want them read by next session."

*Did you know that the average teenager watches three hours of television a day, but talks only an average of five minutes a day with his/her father and seven minutes a day with his/her mother? This means that the average teen spends 15 times more minutes "communicating" with the TV than with parents.** *

*"Behold, I am going to send you Elijah the prophet before the coming of the great and terrible day of the Lord. He will restore the hearts of the fathers to their children and the hearts of the children to their fathers, so that I will not come and smite the land with a curse."*

MALACHI 4:5, 6, NASB.

## TRY IT OUT

1. Start giving hugs to each family member on a regular basis. This includes your aggravating kid brother.

2. When you sense that someone is insecure and your impulse is to steer away from them, go out of your way to say kind and affirming things to them. In some cases they will latch on like a bloodsucker, but you'll be surprised at how many don't.

3. Imagine that you are going to die tomorrow and no one knows but you. Write a letter to each member of your family. What thoughts would you want to leave with them?

## CROSS-EXAMINE THE WITNESS

 *Angela Force is a senior at South Lancaster Academy in Massachusetts. Her heart is really in the West, where there are bigger hills to snowboard on. She plans to be an elementary school teacher because she loves kids.*

QUESTION: WHAT KIND OF FAMILY DO YOU HOPE TO HAVE ONCE YOU HAVE SETTLED DOWN?

I hope to have a husband. Some people might say, "Well, duh!" but in this society it isn't uncommon for a mom to be single. I don't see myself as a single mom. It is not what I want at all. I want a close relationship with my husband, a deep friendship in which we are both comfortable talking and sharing about what our inmost thoughts are. I am human; I have desires, but they are not tantamount to the whole relationship.

I want a home with the traditional dad and mom—but the tradition stops there. In our society the perfect family is made up of four people. Well, I want four *kids*—two boys and two girls. Triplets do run in my family, so I may avoid several pregnancies, which I would not mind at all. I used to have their names picked out, but not anymore. I do want the oldest to be a boy with his father's first name as his middle name.

My home and family would not be complete without at least some kind of pet. Growing up, I had a dog, and they just add so much. A cat would be nice too, but that is my little extra.

I want to be able to talk to my kids when they are teenagers, as my parents are able to talk to me. I want us all to snowboard. I want to keep close ties with my family so my kids can appreciate their aunts, uncles, and grandparents. This goes for my future husband's family too.

I want to be involved in their lives, and watch them experience Jesus for themselves. I want Jesus to be the center of my home, to be the sun around which my family orbits. The Sabbath will be kept, and it will be a time of renewal.

For a sinful world, I have *high* hopes, but I know they are possible with God. My family to come will be nothing without Him anyway. *I* would be nothing without Him.

---

* Mary Pipher, *Reviving Ophelia* (New York: Ballantine Books, 1994), pp. 80-82.

# Popularity

# One of the
# Four Lepers of Samaria

*"We are not doing right. This day is a day of good news, but we are keeping silent; if we wait until morning light, punishment will overtake us. Now therefore come, let us go and tell."*

2 Kings 7:9, NASB.

t's a basic law of economics that the power of money corresponds to how much there is to buy. When there is little of value to buy, money gets weaker and weaker, and it takes more of it to buy things. When there is *nothing* to buy, money has no power at all.

Don't worry; I won't give you a quiz on this. I know it's hard to remember things unless they are relevant to your experience. I could never tell you what I just told you before I saw what I saw in Samaria when Elisha was prophet. In one day, *one* day, our economic condition was turned upside down.

There was famine in the land. I heard that people were selling donkey's heads for what used to buy two yoke of oxen, and a pile of bird dung for the amount that used to buy a whole cageful of doves. Oh, small detail . . . they were eating the stuff! Being a leper, I was intimate enough with poverty to have eaten some pretty vile things, but never pigeon poop!

Then there was the tale of the woman who cooked her son.

No, I didn't say cooked *for* her son; I said *cooked her son*. Scary, huh? I sit in the gate with three other lepers, and we get the town gossip while it's still fresh. This poor starving woman agreed to cook her son one day, and share it . . . *him* . . . with another woman. The other woman was supposed to cook her son the next day and share him. Yes, I'm talking cannibalism. The second woman didn't come through on her end of the bargain. I think God excused her cheating in that case.

King Jehoram was mortified when he heard the story. As is typical of irrational, irreligious people, he blamed the most virtuous person he could find, which in this case was the prophet Elisha.

Elisha had just finished protecting Israel from the Arameans, using his prophetic powers to warn the king of their coming attacks. He had foiled other enemies of Israel, including the fierce Moabites. But even with all the invaluable services Elisha provided, the king's low blood sugar got the better of him that day, and he swore that he would behead the prophet in one cycle of the sundial.

Elisha, upon hearing of this, began to prophesy. He said that by the next day large amounts of fine grain would be sold for pennies in the gate of Samaria. Back to our lesson in economics, it meant that the supply would exceed the demand, and deflation would occur. I looked at my concave stomach and thought, *Fat chance!*

When this pronouncement came, my three leper buddies and I were sitting in the gate, dying. Sounds funny, but it's really true twice over. We faced slow death once when we were diagnosed with leprosy. When the famine came, we were veterans at this looking-death-in-the-eyeball routine. Starving to death? It beats watching your extremities rot! It's better than having rats chew your fingers off while you sleep, because you can't feel them! It's even an improvement on going blind. (When you're a leper, you never moisten your eyes by blinking, and they dry out right in their sockets.) No, death didn't scare us the second time—we actually had kind of a happy-go-lucky attitude about the whole thing. You can't lose something if you ain't got nothin' to lose.

On a candid note, I think the hardest thing about leprosy is becoming an outcast. How can dying physically compare with being told by society that you are an untouchable? Why worry about the death of a body that no one will get near? But it's even more than that, actually. It's that society assumes that your *soul* is also disease-ridden. When people around you tell you often enough that you are a scoundrel, you start to believe popular opinion. The people of our society assumed that leprosy was a punishment for sin, and so according to them, we were not just hopelessly sick, we were hopelessly bad.

The disease, as it progressed, caused the nose and fingers to drop off and the eyelids to disappear. Eventually the breath had a horrible stench, and the flesh grew patches of gray. In the last stages, the nails, teeth, hair, and tongue were eaten alive.

Worst of all, we were to be strictly segregated, away from even our own families. We were to wear torn clothes and let our hair hang loose. And when someone drew near, we were to cry, "Unclean! Unclean!"

I remember the day I left my wife with our three children. "Maybe I will come back someday," I lied, trying to bite back the sobs. She trembled with misery, afraid to embrace me, afraid to let go. I still see them standing there, getting smaller and smaller with each backward glance. There was my beautiful wife, my innocent 7-year-old daughter, and my 13-year-old son on the brink of manhood. Each of their faces was contorted with grief, mouths bent into the same woeful arch, eyes swollen, tears reddening their noses and cheeks with stinging salt. They loved me—oh, how they loved me! But I was unclean, so they couldn't love me anymore.

It's hard to describe the loneliness one feels when cast away from society. You never completely lose your desire to be accepted, but you develop a certain smug attitude toward "those people." In an effort to protect yourself from rejection, you reject them, labeling them outcasts who called you an outcast. You know that in the larger society you could never accomplish this turning of the tables, so you create your own little society with its own rules for acceptance. Normal people become outcasts and lepers become paragons of status. This works well until you have to cry, "Unclean! Unclean!" Somehow shouting those words serves to demolish your self-image every time.

We had a crazy idea as we sat there starving. Why not surrender to Aram? We said, "If they spare us, we live, and if they kill us, the worst thing that can happen is that we die!" At best, we would get a free lunch. At worst, we would hasten the inevitable.

At twilight we walked to the enemy camp. OK, I'll admit that our pulses sped up a bit, that maybe a bead or two of sweat began to stand out on our foreheads. Gradually, though, as we entered the camp, our bodies relaxed when we realized that *no one was there!* We learned later that God had created a sound of thousands of horses galloping, and when the Arameans heard it, they thought a huge army was coming to kill them. Off they ran, leaving behind all their food, clothes, jewelry, equipment, and weapons.

Party time had arrived. One of my buddies grabbed a flask of wine, and another found some roasted meat. Food had never tasted so good, or been eaten so quickly. We began to haul off gold and silver clothes and other priceless treasures we found in the tents. We built a little hiding place off to the side of the camp and began to revel in our newfound riches.

Then conscience kicked in. We thought of the starving people back home, the wives, the children, the other lepers. How could we keep this all to ourselves? True, some of them had treated us as outcasts, but the treasure was much more than we could ever use, especially in what remained of our limited lifetimes. "This is a day of good news," we decided, "but we are keeping silent; if we wait until morning light, punishment will overtake us. Now therefore come, let us go and tell the king's household" (2 Kings 7:9, NASB). And so it was that we went back to Samaria to share our treasures.

When we arrived, we spoke to some high-level town officials. It felt so strange to be talking as equals to men who only hours before were infinitely superior to us. For once we had something to give them besides a disease. Within a few hours the town was filled with Aramean wealth, the people were in high spirits, and we four lepers were celebrities.

In retrospect, though, stardom wasn't all it's cracked up to be. I have come to cherish the thorny side of the path, because it breeds into me a compassion that I would never know if life kept me buoyed up on the waves of popularity.

The same is true for you. You will have your moment in the sun, but probably more moments in the shadows. The question is not "Am I loved?" but "Do I love?" Like us, you will at times be treated as an outcast, and like us, you will at times be a celebrity. Popularity comes and goes, but love never fails.

## COGITATIONS

1. What are the kinds of things that make people popular?

2. Knowing what typically makes a person popular, is it always a worthy pursuit for a Christian? What might be a better pursuit?

3. Jesus went from extreme popularity to the cross. How did He handle praise? reproach?

# What Goes Around Comes Around

*"And Jesus kept increasing in wisdom and stature, and in favor with God and men."*

LUKE 2:52, NASB.

*"If I . . . have not love, I gain nothing."*

1 CORINTHIANS 13:2, NIV.

eceased gangsta rapper Tupac Shakur and Jesus Christ have a few things in common. They were both born into poverty. They both gained great notoriety. They were both murdered in the prime of life.

Tupac's mother was a Black Panther who spent time in jail for a bombing charge while pregnant with him. Tupac's father was shot and killed when he was still a boy. In spite of this legacy of violence, the lad wrote sensitive poetry in school and showed high ideals. Strangely, one poem seems to prophesy an early death:

*In the event of my Demise when my heart can beat no more*
*I Hope I Die For A Principle or A Belief that I had Lived 4*
*I will die Before My Time because I feel the shadow's Depth*
*so much i wanted 2 accomplish before I reached my Death* [1]

Somehow this gentle soul mutated into a violent, aggressive megalomaniac. He carried a gun and shot at people. He was convicted of sexual abuse. His West Coast record label, Death Row, feuded openly and viciously with New York competitor Bad Boy. Just before his death, Shakur and his entourage were accused of beating and stomping a man to death in Las Vegas, where they had come to see a Mike Tyson fight. Not a pretty life.

And the death? Not much prettier. Tupac was riding with Death

Row president Marion Knight in Knight's black BMW after the Tyson fight, standing up through the sunroof when four men rolled up in a white Cadillac, fired about 13 rounds, and drove away. One of his songs was titled "The Streetz R Deathrow," and how well the rapper knew. Apparently he helped make them that way, perhaps at both ends of a gun. So ends the story of Tupac Shakur.

Chuck D, a rapper formerly of the group Public Enemy, thinks that Tupac was a "good brother" gone bad. What made him lose his equilibrium? "Take the high road, and your record never sees the light of day," Chuck says. "Take the low road, and you sell a million copies." [2]

In the hate-based cultures of goth, gangsta rap, and death metal music, we can see a strange phenomenon emerging: Crime is popular; perversity sells. It was once the case that young pop stars were squeaky clean and that part of the criterion for popularity was goodness of character. Somehow in the changes of the past few decades, though, our world has gone mad, and the marketplace has become a bottom-line proof that crime does too pay.

Shakur's popularity was sin-fueled, crime-laden, and short-lived. He will be remembered as a grotesquely violent young man. Thank God, there is another form of popularity. Jesus Christ lived to bless and died to save. He never sinned, and He always loved. Although He suffered mass rejection by His nation and His church, and although His best friends left Him when He needed them most, Jesus has found a place in more hearts than any other figure. Why? Because His character of love survived the test of time. He has forever won the affections of God, angels, and honest human beings the world over, and for this reason Jesus Christ is, in the true sense of the word, popular. This is the kind of popularity God can bless—and there is no crime in it.

## TRY IT OUT

1. Get together with a group of friends, work up your courage, and go out "love bombing." Help elderly women cross the street, hand out flowers to passersby, visit neighbors with small gifts. Some will suspect mischief, but some will receive you gladly.

2. Read the chapter "Before Annas and the Court of Caiaphas" from *The Desire of Ages*. Think about what it must have been like to be rejected by the leaders of your own nation.

3. Find a recording of Handel's *Messiah*. Turn the volume up, close your eyes, lie on your back, and listen to the Hallelujah Chorus and imagine all the millions of people who will one day worship Jesus Christ.

## CROSS-EXAMINE THE WITNESS

*Our witness is Alicia Zimmerman, a home-schooler. She lives with her parents and younger brother in Nepal, which is between India and China. They are missionaries.*

QUESTION: WHAT IS THE DOWN SIDE OF POPULARITY?

My friend was a very shy girl. When she would go to public school, she was not happy, because she just couldn't manage to be outgoing and friendly like the other girls who were very popular. One day when she was riding on the school bus, two boys in front of her were talking. They were some of the most popular boys in the school, whom my friend secretly admired. They said, "You know it is fun to be with these popular girls, but when I get older I'm not going to marry someone like them. I want to marry someone more reserved." My friend thought, *So they don't really respect those girls, but they sure are taking advantage of them and using them as playthings.* She was glad then that she didn't act flirtatious and cheap, as the other girls did.

---

[1] Tupac Shakur, "In the Event of My Demise." www.duke.edu/~del/pacpoem.html

[2] David Van Biema, "'What Goes 'Round . . .'" *Time,* Sept. 23, 1996, p. 40.

# Jepthah

*"For this is the covenant that I will make with the house of Israel after those days, says the Lord: I will put My laws into their minds, and I will write them upon their hearts. And I will be their God, and they shall be My people."*

HEBREWS 8:10, NASB.

hat's up with vows? Jacob vowed to serve God at Bethel, and Hannah vowed that her son would be set aside for God's service. Neither of these vows ended in tragedy, yet my promise to God was a perfect disaster.

Actually, I can see at this point how I was working out of the "old covenant" mind-set.

The old covenant was instituted after Sinai, when the people promised God, "All that the Lord has said we will do, and be obedient!" (Exodus 24:7, NKJV). A short time later they were dancing drunk and naked around a golden calf. So much for human promises.

The point is that when people think they can obey God in their own strength, they make vows that they can't keep. Their frustration mounts, and finally they rebel against Him. Since the time when I made my OC vow (OC stands for old covenant, ironically the same initials as obsessive-compulsive!) I've learned a better option, the new covenant. This is God's promise to me, rather than *my* promise to *Him*. All I do is believe it, deep in my heart.

Then I *want* to obey Him. The difference is that obedience is the *product* of believing that God will save me, rather than a means of coaxing Him to do so. I urge you to live by this new covenant rather than the old, which got me caught in a spider's web of legalism, costing me and my precious daughter very dearly.

You might blame what I did on my psychological baggage, at least in part. Allow me to explain. I was from the family of Gilead, a prominent man in the community who had a slew of sons. This may seem like a "good home" to grow up in, but I was the black sheep of the family. The problem was that my mother was a prostitute, which made me a "son of fornication." Gilead's wife bore him several "real" sons as well. We grew up under the same roof, but when we got old enough to know that we were different, things started getting tense. Finally my half brothers ganged up on me and threw me out of the house.

No one objected to my being homeless, not even my dad. Now, you know what happens to many homeless young men without a father figure—they go bad. I was no exception. I ran with the local renegades, who loved a little violence thrown in with their wine, women, and song. I developed the reputation of being a very tough dude. That's why the elders of the region came to ask my help in fighting the Ammon invasion. A lot of guts those guys had to come crawling after helping my brothers run me out of town!

"Didn't you hate me before when you all drove me away from my father's house?" I asked. "Why are you coming to me now that you're in trouble?"

"If you fight, we will make you head over all of Gilead," they bargained.

"What about if I win the battle for you? Will I still be the prince?" I asked.

"Yes, God is our witness," they promised. "We will do as you have said."

And so I went from social outcast to local hero in a matter of minutes. It wasn't much of a transition in a sense, because I was still in my favorite element—fighting.

## I Want It All

Actually, I tried to be diplomatic and negotiate peace with Ammon, but no deal. I began to psyche myself up for the biggest skirmish of my life. From the deep layers of my soul I felt an energy begin to stir, an energy that would make me larger than life and stronger than a lion. God was with me, I knew it! But I must be honest in saying that I was a mixed bag at that point in my experience. Yes, I wanted to win for God, but mingled into that motivation was a desire to vindicate my own honor. Oh, but how I wanted to earn the respect of the ones who had rejected me, to prove myself worthy to those who had cast me aside as worthless.

So desperately did I long for this battle to be mine that I fell into my old habit patterns and began to bargain with God. The premise of this bargaining was that God would bless me if I blessed Him. It subtly put God on a level with human beings, and ignored the need to trust in Him and submit the outcome of affairs to His wisdom. This for that, tit for tat, eye for eye, tooth for tooth, you scratch my back and I'll scratch yours. A strange way to approach the Creator of the universe, but that's what I did.

"If You give me the Ammonites," I haggled, "I will sacrifice as a burnt offering the first thing that comes out of my door when I return home." I pictured the lambs and goats, my prize possessions, trickling out of the gate at the sound of my steps on the path. They were all I had in terms of wealth, but no price was too high for this victory. At least that's what I thought.

The battle was ours. We rampaged from Aroer to Minnith, 20 cities, and slaughtered them, literally. Oh, it felt so good to feel the admiring eyes upon me as I walked through the crowds of Gileadites, who cheered my once-scorned, now-celebrated name. I soaked it in as any man would, especially a man who had waited his whole life for so much as a shred of recognition. My heart swelled when I saw my brothers—the very ones who had driven me out of my home and nearly out of my mind in the process—looking at me with new respect. Looking closer, I could see in their eyes a touch of shame, no doubt at their earlier treatment of me. Bighearted as I was, I gave them a cheerful wave as I walked by. They seemed relieved.

I made my way home to Mizpah along the familiar road, still soaking in the memory of the postbattle festivities, when my daughter, my one and only child and my heart's delight, came dancing out of the front gate, caught up in the spirit of celebration, tambourines jingling in her delicate hands. I was just at the point of dancing with her when I remembered my vow. My vow! All the euphoria drained out of me in an instant. Tearing my shirt, I cried, "My daughter, my *only* daughter! You have broken my heart! For I promised, I promised . . . I made a promise to God, and I can't take it back!"

Her response was truly amazing. After I apprised her of the situation—sobbing as I did so—she looked off into the distance for a moment as if to come to grips with it all, then riveted her eyes on me and said, "My father, you have given your word to the Lord. Do what you said you would do!" The girl was actually more concerned about my keeping my vows to God than she was about her own life!

"But leave me alone for two months," she continued, "and let me go to the mountains with my friends and weep. I will never be married, Father. How sad! Let me mourn for two months before you fulfill your vow."

So my girl—my pretty, young, fresh, unspoiled girl—left for two months to mourn the tragedy of her life and mine. Sad to say, even with two months to think it over, I still felt I had to fulfill the vow I had made. I rationalized that my whole family, including my daughter, would suffer the wrath of God if I didn't keep it, so she would be sacrificed in one way or another.

Oh, if I only knew then what I know now. If only I had been willing to treat God as God and exercise faith in Him, rather than thinking I had to bid for every blessing. I now see the battle with Ammon as a symbol of the larger battle between good and evil. God has already promised victory, a victory He Himself will give. Why should we bargain for what's already ours? Why not just thank Him for His generosity? If I had done so, I might now have grandchildren to cheer me in my old age.

*(Get the story of Jepthah for yourself in Judges 11 and*
Patriarchs and Prophets, *page 558.)*

## COGITATIONS

1. Have you ever made a promise to God that you failed to keep? How did you feel once you failed?

2. Is there a difference between a commitment and a promise? If so, what is it?

3. Humanity's covenants are two-sided, while God's covenant with Abraham in Genesis 17:1-8 seems rather one-sided, God doing all the promising. What is the significance of this?

4. While the covenant of Abraham was based on God's promise and not Abraham's, God did ask for a response from Abraham. What was it? What response that He asks from us today is symbolized?

# A Herd of Virgins

Virginity pledges are a good thing. A movement has been afoot in our country since about 1993 called True Love Waits, which leads teenagers to commit to sexual abstinence until marriage. The movement has made its impact—a high-profile study proved that teenagers who publicly promise to postpone sex until marriage refrain substantially (a year and a half, on average) longer than teens who didn't make such a pledge.[1]

But there are caveats. The program works better for younger kids, ages 15 and 16, than older kids. Looking at this fact in the context of caveat number two indicates that what makes the "Love Waits" pledges work is the herd mentality of younger kids, a mentality that dissipates for older teens when they learn to make decisions for themselves. You see, the study discovered that kids typically made these pledges in groups, and kept the pledges as long as the group was neither too large nor too small. When the group got too large, the kids lost their sense of being part of a "special" clique; when it got too small, the fear of being "weird" proved their undoing. As long as it was "cool" to be virgin, the program worked, but when it became "uncool," resolve weakened, and kids began to break their vows.[2]

Is there a way to keep a young person clean whether it's cool or not? Will the coming and going of popular opinion and peer fear always have the final word? Yes to the first question, no to the second. There is a better way, and it's called faith. By faith Noah built an ark to a chorus of teasing that lasted 120 years. By faith Moses refused the prestige of being the prince of Egypt, so he could suffer with God's people. By faith Rahab risked her life to help God's spies. These and others resisted the pull of popularity and the fear of ridicule, because they lived by faith in God's promises.

Virginity pledges work, but they work best for certain kids under certain conditions. Faith works for tempted sinners of *any* age under *all* conditions. God can keep you pure through belief in His promises. But a caution is in order—make sure that the faith you have is the real thing, not the cheap counterfeit that makes "the devils . . . believe, and tremble" (James 2:19). The imps of hell have an intellectual grasp of the facts, but no heart-changing, dynamic faith that works by love. A goblin's grasp of the gospel won't do you any good when it comes to the powerful temptation of immorality. The crucible of the strongest temptation holds the fire that shows faith for what it is—either intellectual-checklist faith or the real thing. Get down on your knees and make sure you have the right kind.

*"It is better to take refuge in the Lord than to trust in man. It is better to take refuge in the Lord than to trust in princes."*

PSALM 118:8, 9, NASB.

# I Want It All

*"Therefore, since Christ has suffered in the flesh, arm yourselves also with the same purpose, because he who has suffered in the flesh has ceased from sin, so as to live the rest of the time in the flesh no longer for the lusts of men, but for the will of God."*

1 PETER 4:1, 2, NASB.

## TRY IT OUT

1. Read *Patriarchs and Prophets,* pages 370-372. Put in your own words the difference between the new and the old covenants.

2. Read the Ten Commandments in Exodus 20:1-17, but notice the second verse in chapter 20: "I am the Lord your God, who brought you out of the land of Egypt, out of the house of slavery" (NASB). God reminds of the fact that He has freed us from slavery before He asks us to obey Him. Meditate on this fact.

3. Now read the commandments as 10 promises rather than 10 rules.

## CROSS-EXAMINE THE WITNESS

 **Our witness is Kimberly Dawn Schwirzer, a junior high student from Connecticut. Kimmy is only four feet five inches tall, but she makes up for it with a larger-than-life personality.**

QUESTION: HOW HAS THE NEW COVENANT BECOME A REALITY IN YOUR LIFE

The new covenant helps me realize that we are very important to God. This makes me want to make Him important in my life. A lot of us give in to temptation because we don't believe. "For God so loved the world that He gave His only begotten Son, that whoever believes in Him should not perish but have everlasting life" (John 3:16, NKJV). The condition for eternal life is believing. Believing, though, does *not* lead me to procrastinate; it leads me to repent for my sins now and obey God today.

I used to be afraid of the time of trouble, but now I am not afraid, because I trust that God knows what's best for me. Sometimes I go off and on with fighting the temptations of everyday life, but in the end I have faith that I'll pull through if I continue to believe God's promise to me.

---

[1] Jessica Reaves, "The Good (and Bad?) News About Virginity Pledges," www.time.com/time/education/article/0,8599,93958,00.html.

[2] *Ibid.*

# Hushai the Archite

*"A friend loves at all times, and a brother is born for adversity."*

PROVERBS 17:17, NASB.

Shhhh . . . quiet. Isn't it ironic that I, being a spy, have that command smack dab in the middle of my name? Shhhh . . . Hushhhhhh . . . Hushhhhhhai . . . Hushhhai the Archite, professional snoop, sleuth, and government informant—that's me.

Affection and disaffection. Honor and dishonor. Loyalty and betrayal. You name it: All the great contrasts were involved in the great rebellion. Family and friendship ties were either proven or broken, made stronger or shattered beyond repair. As for me, I'm happy to say I got some lifelong friends out of the experience, one of them being King David.

It all started with the prince. Absalom was a gorgeous-looking fellow who towered above most and looked down upon all. He had distinct features, a strong chin, a high forehead. And the hair! I've never seen such a mass of wavy blackness. Every year he was forced to cut it because of the sheer weight that pulled on his neck. He would proudly weigh the hair, which averaged 200 shekels, the weight of a large pot of olive oil. When you added it all together—hair, the height, and the glorious face—no matter what angle you looked at the guy, he was a picture of perfection. But there was something deceptive about it all. Physical beauty is, in a sense, a reflection of the beauty of God. So when you see a good-looking person, you're tempted to invest them with virtue of character. With Absalom, this proved to be a fatal assumption.

I watched the insurrection from the beginning. David had sunk into a real funk after his affair with Bathsheba. As much as God forgave him, he still reaped the results of his actions in a damaged conscience and a disillusioned kingdom. Foremost among the ones disaffected by his crime was Ahithophel, one of the most prominent scholars of Israel, a great and respected mind and no less than Bathsheba's grandfather. This brainiac of a guy was as complex emotionally as he was brilliant intellectually, and he never could forgive David for what he had done.

The rebellion came as a surprise to David, even though it had been brewing for years. Absalom had been deported for three years for murder conspiracy. When he was finally allowed back into the kingdom, David still held him at arm's length. This was a real blunder on David's part, because while he brooded in his palace, Absalom schmoozed with the people, acting as counselor, sympathizer, advocate, and fellow party animal. Before long he was at the center of stardom, high in the affections of the people, and in a prime position to usurp the throne.

The coup came the day Absalom announced that he was going to a religious ceremony in Hebron, 20 miles from Jerusalem. Two hundred men went with him, thinking they were following a pious man on the way to worship God. When the prince arrived in Hebron, he called Ahithophel, who drew hundreds more influential men from around the kingdom into the conspiracy. The trumpet of revolt was sounded.

Because David knew he had brought the crisis upon himself, he had a very humble attitude as he packed to leave Jerusalem. He wasn't without loyal followers, mind you. There was even a group of 600 converted pagans who went with him. The priests came with the ark, which David subsequently made them take back. And then there was me.

David had been told about the defection of Ahithophel, and when he reached the top of Mount Olivet, he bowed in prayer. That's when I found him, with my robes torn and dirt on my head. David saw in me an immediate answer to prayer and an instrument through which he could fight the rebellion.

"If you return to the city as a spy," he said, "you may be able to thwart Ahithophel's counsel for me! Zadok and Abiathar the priests will be there as well. We can set up a line of communication, from Absalom's counsels to you, to the priests. Then they can communicate to their sons, who can bring the message to us!" It seemed to be a watertight plan.

Back to the city I went, just in time to see Absalom pompously promenading into Jerusalem as if he owned the place. Now was the time to use my acting skills.

"Long live the king! Long live the king!" I shouted in his hearing.

Absalom looked pleased. "Why didn't you go with your friend?" he said, as if bating me to denounce David.

"No!" I shouted. "God and this people have chosen *you* to rule over them, and so will I!"

What followed tested my theatrical ability even more than lavishing approval upon the brat prince. I had to stifle my reaction of disgust to one of the most disgraceful things I have ever heard. At Absalom's request Ahithophel gave him the following counsel:

"Go in to your father's concubines. This will make your father hate you and your people love you all the more!"

I tried not to show my nausea. Ahithophel had never been a man of great virtue, but this was adultery and incest all in one revolting package. Yet the man's counsel was so respected it was as if one had inquired of God Himself. And so it was done. A tent was pitched for Absalom on the roof, the same roof from which David had spied Bathsheba, and there in front of all Israel he went in to the king's concubines.

Athithophel had more counsel. "Please give me 12,000 men so that I can pursue David tonight," he schemed. "I will come upon him while he is weary and exhausted, and I will frighten his men away and kill him. Then I will bring the people back to you."

Tension mounted. Absalom was pleased, but I wasn't, because I knew full well that if the prince followed the counsel of Ahithophel, David was history. Fortunately, Absalom wanted to know what *I* thought about the plan.

*"This* time," I began, trying to sound as if I agreed with Ahithophel most of the time, "the advice of Ahithophel isn't good. You know your father and his men—they are as violent as a bear robbed of her cubs! What's more, your father won't sleep with the people, but will be in hiding somewhere. If our people attack, David will counterattack, and it will strike terror to the hearts of our soldiers! I counsel you to gather all of Israel to yourself and that *you* go into battle with them."

The next span of time found me crying out to God from the bottom of my soul. *O, God, please have him follow my advice . . .* God doesn't always answer my prayers, but this time He did. Absalom reassembled the counsel and said, "The advice of Hushai the Archite is better than the counsel of Ahithophel."

The next string of events remind me of some kind of camel trader's folklore.

I told the priests, who told a maidservant, who told the priest's sons, who were supposed to go tell David. A young boy from the rebellion saw the priest's sons, and told Absalom. So the priest's sons hid in the well of a man named Bahurim, whose wife spread a covering over the well and scattered grain on it. When Absalom's servants came, this brave lady said that the men had crossed a brook. When the servants left, the priest's sons ran and warned David to cross the Jordan before Absalom got him. David took every last one of the loyals, women and children included, and crossed the mighty, swift flowing river in the dark of night.

Meanwhile, back at the palace, Ahithophel was distraught that his advice was not followed. He knew that David would win the battle. Absalom would be forgiven, of course. But Atithophel knew he wouldn't be so lucky, because he had counseled the prince to commit incest and adultery. He would probably face the stoning pit, the gallows, or death by the sword. Knowing all this, Ahithophel went home, put his affairs in order, and hanged himself before David could get to him.

The battle was indeed won, and we returned to Jerusalem. Reclining in the palace, I couldn't help but remark at the strange twist of events that had taken place. When David was hunted like an animal, I elected to be the friend that he needed. Oh, sure, the guy had failed us miserably when he fell with Bathsheba and committed murder to cover it up. Even after his great repentance, he was still falling short of the kind of leadership we all needed in Israel. But he needed a friend. I was honored to be that friend in his great day of adversity. It was a risk to help him, but if I had to choose between life knowing that I had failed him, and death knowing I hadn't, I would choose death. Fortunately, I got the best of both worlds.

*(Get the story of Hushai for yourself in 2 Samuel 15; 16:15-23; and 17; and* Patriarchs and Prophets, *pages 735-741.)*

## COGITATIONS

1. Is there anyone in your life who took a great risk to remain loyal to you? How have you expressed appreciation to them, if at all?

2. We might not engage in physical war, but there are social and spiritual wars between people all around us. Is there always a good guy and a bad guy, or can the line be kind of fuzzy?

3. Both Ahithophel and Absalom had charisma and power. What was it based upon? Are there people in our world who have the same kind of power for the same reasons? What will eventually happen to their influence?

4. Everyone who was loyal to David in this story ran the risk of being on the losing side. How does this apply to the great controversy between Christ and Satan?

# The Gossip of the Goblins

wo goblins sat together by the side of the highway of life conversing with each other.

"I have noticed something about the goblin who lives next to me," said the older of the two. His face was twisted into a perpetual sneer, and large coarse hairs stood out from his chin, poking the air as he spoke. "He has hair on his chin!"

The younger of the two seemed energized by this tidbit and quickly responded, "Yes, that disgusting hair on his chin!" He didn't seem to realize that he spoke to someone with hair much coarser and uglier, or even that as he spoke he stroked his own hair-laden chin.

"What really turns my stomach, though, is the warts!" said the older through slimy lips. At that moment he wrinkled his nose, and his own large, gray-green wart twitched like a bug on a bedpost.

"Oh, yeah!" said the young goblin. "Warts really turn me off!" He waved his wart-encrusted hand with an air of superiority as if to shoo away a fly.

Neither seemed aware of his own warts. In fact, at the moment these warts were mentioned as being on a goblin not present, the conversing goblins became blind to those very blemishes upon themselves.

So it was with the next criticism. "You know what I really hate?" said the young goblin, seeming anxious to impress the older with his fine sensibilities.

"Yeah, I know—*bad breath!*" said the older, rolling back in laughter that stretched his stomach skin to a shiny taut. The other instantly joined him, throwing his knobby head back and releasing with each guffaw a stench so vile it might have been used in chemical warfare. In fact, because of the increased vocal exercise of laughter, a cloud of gaseous filth surrounded both goblins, emerging up from the pit of their sour stomachs and out of their germ-infested mouths.

But as far as they were concerned, there was only sweetness in their midst.

And so the conversation continued, defect after defect being pointed out on the goblins not present, and defect after defect on the goblins who spoke of them seemingly vanishing into thin air. At last the two goblins appeared—in their own eyes, that is—with perfect, dewy skin, proportionate features, symmetrical bodies, luxuriant hair, sweet-smelling breath, and a fine, prideful sparkle in their eyes.

But in fact, as they strode together down the highway, they were two of the ugliest, most foul-smelling creatures that could be found.

Such is the nature of gossip. We do it to make ourselves appear lovely to ourselves and others. But although in gossiping, our warts may disappear from our own eyes, they remain, in the eyes of God, warts—all the uglier because we think we have them not.

*"No one can tame the tongue; it is a restless evil and full of deadly poison."*

JAMES 3:8, NASB.

# The Treason of the Trolls

several trolls sat, all fat and dumpy, at a large table in a dimly lit underground room. The subject was a fellow troll—in fact the chief of the trolls—not present who had allegedly violated the troll bylaws and guidelines by neglecting to pay his yearly troll tax. This tax was used for the upkeep of the town, and it was thought that a troll chief who failed to pay his due would set a precedent that would lead the entire troll population into tax fraud.

"Corruption in high places," intoned an old troll with white fuzzy hair atop his deeply wrinkled head, "will lead to anarchy! Order must be maintained!" With these words, spoken as loudly as his frail voice would allow, the old troll pounded the table, unfortunately missing the table on the last pound, which sent him toppling to the floor. Several trolls came to his aid, helping him back into his chair and brushing him off carefully.

Sitting at the opposite end of the table was a younger troll with a significantly stronger build, if a troll can ever be said to have a strong build. Let's just say that somehow the ripples of his fat were a little less flaccid than the other trolls' ripples. Likewise, his voice had a clearer tone. Seeing the old troll propel himself to the floor had brought forth in this troll so strong an urge to laugh that he had to place his fat hand across his mouth and furrow his brow as if in deep thought to mask it. Once this troll's composure was fully regained, he was ready to speak.

"Immediate, decisive action must be taken. To fail to act is to act irresponsibly. In this day of crisis I propose that we form a new government, headed of course by a new chief . . ."

All the while this stronger troll spoke, there was a quiet, small troll who sat in the corner of the table saying nothing. The silence of his lips, however, was in sharp contrast to the violent argument going on in his mind. He heard the words of the strong troll, interpreting them to his own dilemma: "To fail to act is to act irresponsibly . . . to fail to act is to act irresponsibly . . . to fail to act . . ."

This troll had a secret that he feared to share because of the possibility of being scorned and ridiculed. He knew that the chief troll had *not* failed to pay his tax at all. He knew that the chief had, in fact, made great sacrifices in helping poor trolls in *addition* to his faithful taxpaying. He also knew that the strong troll had instigated the rumor of tax fraud, creating his own opportunity to seize the leadership position. It was all a scheme, a stinking subterfuge concocted out of a cocky cranium full of crock.

And the quiet troll knew it. And the quite troll *stayed* quiet.

And the whole troll patrol took control and stole the role of the chief troll for failing to pay his troll toll. And throughout the whole troll rigmarole the quiet troll stayed . . . quiet.

*"[There is] a time to be silent and a time to speak."*

ECCLESIASTES 3:7, NASB.

## TRY IT OUT

1. Often words hurt more than they heal. Put yourself in touch with the power of words with a "talking fast" for a day, or even an hour. See if you can get some others to do it with you, perhaps a class at school.

2. Make a point of looking for opportunities to say good things about people who are being gossiped about. Do this for a day. When you hear bad things being said, praise something in that person's life or character.

3. Split a paper into two columns. Head one column "builders" and one "wreckers." List the things that build or wreck friendship in their respective columns, then compare yourself with the list. Are there things you could do to build relationships? Are there ways in which you are wrecking them?

# CROSS-EXAMINE THE WITNESS

 *Our witness is Earl James Noble, a part-time student living in St. John's, Newfoundland, Canada. He spends too much time on the computer, plays piano, sings solos (that no one can hear but him), and loves photography and sports. He also loves writing, as you will see.*

QUESTION: EARL, HOW DOES THE GOOD NEWS OF THE GOSPEL AFFECT YOUR RELATIONSHIPS WITH OTHER PEOPLE?

To use a comparison, I'd like you to think about two people. One person is a Christian trying to live for God in every way. The other person is your "ordinary Joe," going to church maybe once or twice a year, at Christmas and Easter, but who is otherwise too consumed in the world to think much about God. Now throw in a middle-aged, homeless person, who is merely down on his luck.

Who do you think would be able to make friends with this man first—the person living for God, or the person trying to hail a cab before getting a little windblown? This illustration makes you think twice about what's going on in your life, doesn't it?

How many people have you not bothered to try to make friends with just because you didn't think it was worth the trouble? Maybe the best friend you could ever have was right under your nose but slipped away because you didn't want to put forth the effort of simply talking to them.

If you look at the big picture, it comes down to one point. The closer you are to God, the closer you are able to become to others, because the love of God will flow through you into them, then from them back into you. It will make you both feel better, because everyone could use a little loving every now and then.

# Samson's Ex

*"You are our letter, written in our hearts, known and read by all men."*

2 Corinthians 3:2, NASB.

The first view I had of my now-ex-husband was the day he decided to marry me. If that isn't love at first sight, I don't know what is. Yes, I have been told all my life that I'm beautiful, and I can't deny that it's true—something had to make me stand out in a crowd to Samson of Zorah, the man everyone was talking about. He had fraternized with the Philistines from the time he was a kid, even though he himself was a Nazirite—a special sect among the worshipers of Jehovah. Through my oh-so-brief, turbulent marriage to Samson I got firsthand exposure to these people who claim to worship the one true God. I don't know about that God. Judging by the behavior of Samson, He can't be very true at all.

After meeting me, Samson went home to his parents and demanded that they arrange for our marriage. This was a real problem because marriage with those outside their faith was against policy, and probably for good reason. They pleaded with him to pick a wife from among their own people, but he insisted on me, saying, "Get her for me; she's good-looking!" Obviously physical attraction was number one on his list of priorities in choosing a wife. None of the girls from his religion really turned him on, so he chose me against his parents' wishes. Their own commandments state that children should honor their parents, but in Samson's case the roles were reversed. The parents ultimately did what the child wanted. He was a master manipulator!

The family left for my home in Timnah so we all could meet. On the way Samson accomplished his legendary slaying of the lion with his bare hands. Passing by the carcass of the lion again on his way to our wedding feast, Samson saw that some bees had made a nest inside, which was dripping with honey. This event gave him a basis for a riddle that he would use later to trick my countrymen out of some of their possessions.

"Let me give you a riddle," he announced at the weeklong wedding reception. "If you guess it within these seven days, I will give you 30 complete suits of clothing. If you can't guess it, you give me 30 complete suits of clothing." Thirty outfits! We were talking high stakes.

My brothers grimaced a little, knowing what a conniving type Samson was, but they dared not appear wimpy and refuse the challenge. "Propound your riddle!" they shouted.

Suddenly the general pandemonium ceased, and all eyes fastened upon Samson. With a smile of pleasure at being the center of attention, he spoke: "Out of the eater came something to eat, and out of the strong came something sweet."

Eyes darted back and forth and the guessing, which continued almost nonstop for three full days, began. "Dates imported from Egypt!" "Persimmons from Persia!" "A new kind of cow with edible doo-doo!" Each guess snapped all heads in the direction of Samson, who, with a perpetual expression of smugness on his face, replied, "No, no, no," every time.

Finally it wasn't funny anymore. On the fourth day of the feast the men cornered me with a demand that sent shivers up my spine. "Get the answer for us, girl," they said. "Wheedle, coax, seduce, whatever you have to do, but get it. If you don't, we will burn your father's house to the ground with you in it. Did you bring us to this wedding to inflict us with poverty?"

*Fascinating challenge,* I thought. *Manipulating the master manipulator! I wonder if I can do it.* As much out of ambition as out of fear of getting torched, I set out to get the answer. What method would I employ? It didn't take long for me to arrive at a strategy—I would use the favorite last-resort weapon of all womankind and the only thing more powerful than a woman's beauty. I would use a beautiful woman's *tears.*

"You hate me!" I sobbed to a bewildered-looking Samson in our tent that night. "You don't love me! If you loved me you would have no secrets, and you have not told me the answer to your riddle!"

"I haven't even told my parents! Why should I tell you?" he said, frowning. In spite of his backsliding, he retained a certain loyalty to Israel, and a certain separateness from me. It was as if I couldn't really be trusted. How could I blame him? I couldn't!

For the next several days I continued my weeping and wailing until the last day of the feast. The strong man's nerves were frayed into threads by this time, and he finally snapped. The answer to the riddle: the lion with the honey inside. *How ironic, pushover Samson,* I thought. *Just like you—a powerful beast with soft, gooey innards.*

Once informed, the men cornered Samson. "What is sweeter than honey?" they asked with a sneer. "And what is stronger than a lion?"

Without missing a beat, Samson shot back another riddle, a riddle they couldn't help understanding. "If you had not plowed with my heifer, you would not have guessed my riddle." I still don't know if I'm comfortable with the heifer metaphor.

What came next was more spectacular than the original lion-slaying. Samson experienced that divine empowerment that had made him the talk of the land. Filled with the Spirit of his God, Samson traveled to Ashkelon and killed 30 men. This wasn't pure retaliation, although that element was present. Samson reasoned that he was merely obtaining the payment for a bet won by fraud from the very people who defrauded him. The Philistine men won 30 suits of clothes through unfair means. Samson would deliver on his end of the bargain by getting the 30 suits off 30 dead Philistines. This event made me realize that, as wedded as he was to our country through me, he was still the enemy of the Philistines.

That was some time ago. Samson disappeared for a while,

and it was assumed that he was breaking his engagement with me. My father married me off to another man a short time later. How do I feel about my new circumstances? Life has been boring, to say the least.

The exciting news is that Samson showed up again today in Timnah. He brought a young goat as a gift and told my father that he was going into my room to give it to me. That's when dad broke the news that I had been remarried. "I thought you hated her after she betrayed you," he said. My father proceeded to point to my younger sister, trying to auction her off to the guy with the bulging pectoral muscles. He kept saying, "She's more beautiful, don't you think?" I'm still feeling insulted.

That was a few hours ago. Since then, pure chaos has broken out in Timnah because of what Samson did next. Apparently, he has burned to the ground our entire ripe harvest of grain, along with all of our grapes and fruit trees. Smoke is everywhere, and men are running around trying to scrape together enough sand to smother what is left of the fires, but it's hopeless. My father told me that Samson took 30 foxes, tied them into couples by the tails, fastened a torch on each one, and let them loose on our farms. I wonder what we will eat this year.

Samson! Samson! I loved you in the most passionate, dysfunctional way. What is left for me to enjoy since I have had the pleasure of being loved and lusted for by you? But I guess the union was doomed from the beginning. We came from different worlds, different faiths. As easily as you were led astray you kept going back to the God of your fathers. I don't know about that God—I judged Him by looking at you. Did you give me the right picture?

Even as I write, I see several Philistine men coming with torches. I wonder what's left to burn?

*(Get the story of Samson's ex for yourself in Judges 14; 15:1-6;*
*and* Patriarchs and Prophets, *pages 560-563.)*

## COGITATIONS

1. If a non-Christian judged God's character by looking at you, what conclusions would they come to?

2. Samson entered into friendships with the Philistines, but it did not lead to their conversion to the true God. Why was Samson's witness so weak? How can we best befriend people in a way that will draw them to Jesus?

3. God warns us against being "unequally yoked" with unbelievers in unions such as marriage (2 Corinthians 6:14). Why do you think He does this?

# Head, Shoulders, Knees, and Toes

*"For the body is not one member, but many."*

1 CORINTHIANS 12:14, NASB.

God describes His church in terms of body parts. "What good" He asks, "are hands, feet, heads, ears, eyes, and noses that think they don't need each other?" (my own synopsis of 1 Corinthians 12:12-27). At best they are useless; at worst they are *grotesque*. (Have you ever seen an eyeball all by itself?)

What is needed to get God's body parts in good working order is cooperation. Our body parts don't have a free will, but God's body parts do. We body parts must cooperate in two ways: with God, and with each other.

The reason God's body, the church, is so fragmented, is that we are out of sync with Him. The church exists because of truth—and since there is only one truth, there should be only one church. Instead, there are many churches, and even within one church there are many beliefs. When the Holy Spirit fell at Pentecost, the disciples were "all with one accord in one place" (Acts 2:1). This doesn't mean they were all stuffed into one Honda, but that they all believed the same thing. They had consensus, and their consensus was correct. Jesus Christ was the crucified and risen Messiah. By the way—don't think it was as easy to be a Christian then as it is now. In those days, Christian churches were burned. Today they receive tax exemptions. It cost them much to believe in Jesus, yet they believed still.

What can individuals do without the cooperation of the body? They can make a show of religion, but it means little or nothing. Consider Amar Bharti of India. He claims that he kept his right hand elevated for 26 years as a gesture of devotion to the Hindu god Shiva. His fingers have withered into the palm of his hand, his knuckles are white with rot, and his nails have grown long and twisted. A strange form of witnessing, to say the least.[1]

And then there is Arthur Blessitt of North Fort Myers, Florida. He has walked a longer distance than any other human being—33,151 miles as of the year 2000. The remarkable thing about his journey is that he has carried a wooden cross the entire time, presumably to witness of his religion to onlookers.[2]

As dedicated as these individuals are, neither Amar's hand or Arthur's feet can really convince the world of the truth. We are God's hands and feet, but we work His will only when we are connected to each other and to Him. Jesus said, "By this all men will know that you are My disciples, if you have love for one another" (John 13:35, NASB). No one can accomplish alone what God said must be accomplished as a cooperative unit. No matter how you size it up, body parts working out of harmony with each other will never accomplish God's mission for His church.

But neither will God working alone. According to the Bible, the head (Jesus) does not say to the feet, "I have no need of you"

(1 Corinthians 12:21, NASB). *What? God needs us?* Apparently so. *For what?* To share the truth about Him with the world. The proof of our message is love and cooperation between His body parts. Oh, we who are called to be God's hands—can we grasp it?

---

[1] *Guinness Book of World Records 2000* (Stamford, Conn.: Guinness World Records Ltd., 2000), p. 51.

[2] *Ibid.,* p. 54.

# Steal Away

 twentysomething White male with a stab wound to the chest was brought into the ER with a scarlet trail behind him. The trauma surgeon thought that the heart had probably been penetrated, and that in addition to needing a blood transfusion, the patient needed his chest cracked (heart surgery).

One of the nurses spoke: "This patient can't be given any blood. He's a Jehovah's Witness. It's right here in his wallet!" She held up a card.

Silence fell upon the room. Nurses and medics glanced around nervously until the surgeon spoke. "Let's get that O-negative blood up here," he barked.

The nurse objected, "I said he doesn't want any blood. I'm a Jehovah's Witness too. You know our belief about blood transfusions. I won't let you give that patient blood!"

Doctor and nurse were now face to face. "If this guy doesn't get any blood," the doctor said, "he'll certainly die no matter what we do. You know every second counts."

The nurse stood her ground, saying, "If you give him the blood, he would rather be dead. He signed this card. You have to honor his wish."

Since no blood had arrived yet anyway, the surgeon opened

the boy's chest and began operating on his heart, but the injuries were too extensive, too serious. The boy died before they could get a blood transfusion even near him.

Later in the evening, when the police arrived, it was found that the young stab wound victim was not a Jehovah's Witness at all. He had stolen the wallet.*

But what if the boy could have been saved by a blood transfusion? Would he have died a Jehovah's Witness, not really being one?

Stolen religion is worse than no religion at all. Make sure you have your own. It's a matter of life and death.

*"While you have the light, believe in the light, that you may become sons of light."*

JOHN 12:36, NKJV.

## TRY IT OUT

Have you ever done a trust fall? Ask your gym teacher or another leader if you can try it. A group stands behind a person who is standing on the edge of a table. The group is in two rows, ready to catch the person as they fall. The person—they can be forward or backward—falls into the arms of the group. This exercise can actually teach a person to fall properly, lessening their chances of injury if they fall accidentally.

## CROSS-EXAMINE THE WITNESS

*Our witness is Adel Arrabito, a student at Pacific Union College in California. Adel grew up in a family that was dedicated to ministry. She has a special talent for moving her ears and making people laugh, but what she has to share with us is very serious.*

QUESTION: WHEN DID YOU MAKE YOUR RELIGION YOUR OWN?

# I Want It All

The death of my father and brothers in a tragic plane crash led to my conversion. Let me tell you the story.

I remember sitting with my head resting heavily on my mother's shoulder. My brother's head rested on the other shoulder, and both of us were crying bitterly. My mind spun as the words echoed through my head, but the tears would not come.

"Daddy and Tony and Joey are dead, aren't they?" my brother had asked Mom after she came in from talking to the pastor.

"Yes, Daddy and Tony and Joey are dead."

That was when my head dropped, but the words continued to go around in my 8-year-old head as my whole being screamed, "No, it can't be!" When the tears finally came, they would not be stopped. My daddy and two dear brothers were gone from my life, and I could not imagine ever being happy again.

The months and years that followed that horrible night were long and lonely. I shut out my loss and wondered where God was. I didn't know how to make friends, and I felt like a reject. A night of truth came when I was 14, and I gave my life completely to the Great Comforter. My life has never been perfect, but I've come to understand something: God's way is perfect, and no matter what happens in life, He can bring good from it. Once my life was in His hands, I knew I would never face danger or hardship alone. God does not change with the circumstances. He is always greater than them.

---

* Adapted from Mark Brown, *Emergency! True Stories From the Nation's ERs* (New York: Villard Books, 1996) pp. 56-58.

# Romance

# Abigail

*"For your husband is your Maker, whose name is the Lord of hosts; and your Redeemer is the Holy One of Israel, who is called the God of all the earth."*

ISAIAH 54:5, NASB.

I was as thrilled as any young girl would be when my father announced that a husband had been chosen for me. Nabal was his name, a wealthy shepherd from Maon, a descendant of the brave and virtuous Caleb. "Nabal, Nabal," I repeated over and over, savoring the sound. I envisioned a tall, handsome fellow lavishing me day and night with tokens of noble affection.

On my wedding night I cried myself to sleep, beginning a trend that would continue for all the years I was with him. He was a harsh, evil-tempered wino with disgusting manners and fewer tender emotions than a wild boar.

But God saw to it that my misery ended, or at least changed into a different form. My story is one of disappointed hopes ending in a dream come true. Unfortunately, there is a postscript: more disappointed hopes. Between my two marriages I learned that often life gives you only two choices; you can either have a slob to yourself or share a prince with others. Read on; you'll see what I mean.

Things were not happy in our home. Out of loyalty to Nabal I tried to smooth over the havoc he wreaked in his business and personal relationships. The man just did not have a civil bone in his body. At times I considered leaving him, but where would I have gone? If a girl had money to buy wheat for breadmaking and a new robe every year, she was considered fortunate. My parents simply would not consent to my return home for reasons of emotional emptiness. So I stayed, dutiful and miserable.

Some wayfaring men came to the house one day to ask for provisions, claiming that David, the future king of Israel, was their leader. They pointed out that they had been in proximity to Nabal's shepherds in Carmel and had protected them, refraining from the thievery of which travelers were often guilty. I'm sure they were expecting a gracious thank-you in the form of some bread, wine, and dried fruits. This would have been the customary courtesy, but that expectation was based on an ignorance of the character of my husband.

"Who is David?" Nabal began his usual put-down routine. "The wilderness is full of fugitive slaves and other no-accounts. Should I become a welfare center for a bunch of unknowns?"

A bit shocked and humbled, David's servants left. I thought I might hear of the travelers robbing a few shepherds after that, but I never expected David to attempt the revenge that he did. A short time later he and 400 of his men came swinging their swords, looking for us all. They were bent upon wiping out the entire family of my madman husband. It wasn't the first time my identification with him proved a risk! And it wasn't the first time I tried to effect peace.

I took 200 loaves of bread, two barrels of wine, five roasted sheep, several bags of roasted grain, 100 clusters of raisins, and 200 cakes of figs and loaded them onto donkeys. The plan was that my young men servants would go before me and I would follow with the food. Nabal had no idea, for if I had told him, he would have forbidden it and then brought war to his household and probably death to himself.

My first close-up look at David was from the ground. After riding until I spotted him and his 400, I had fallen on my face before him in a gesture of humility, hoping to assuage his anger. Lifting my face, I opened my mouth to begin my peace negotiations with one of the most handsome men I have ever laid eyes on.

"Let the blame fall on me!" I pleaded. "Listen to me. My husband is named Nabal, which means 'folly,' and that's exactly what he is—a fool! I didn't see the young men when they came asking for food, or I would have seen to it that they received some." I let David know that I knew he was God's man, the future king of Israel. He seemed to appreciate it.

"Blessed be the Lord God of Israel, who sent you this day to meet me," he said with a soft look, "and you are blessed as well. If you had not stopped me, not one man of the household of Nabal would have been left." By now my heart was thumping like a bass drum. There was between us a certain eye contact, an instant intimacy, even though we were several feet apart, that cut through everything in our surroundings. It was as if we were together on some other plane, alone, although in reality surrounded with onlookers. Love at first sight, I think they call it.

I rode back home on cloud nine, a cloud that evaporated as soon as Nabal appeared before me. He was feasting with his drunken cronies and quite drunk himself. Not a good time to tell him he had just been saved from the sword.

I went to bed that night with a head full of questions. "Why, God, do I have this son of Belial for a husband? Why did You give me this intelligent mind, this heart that yearns for tenderness, then lock me in with such a brute? Why, oh, why couldn't I be married to someone like David?" I hugged my pillow and cried myself to sleep.

Morning came, and with it the shocking answer to my prayers. Nabal had quite a hangover, but was steady on his feet, so I let him know what I had saved him from the day before. Some might have accused me of purposely shocking him to death, but I had no idea that his reaction would be so severe. He collapsed in front of me. After a 10-day coma he was gone, and I was free. The fact that I regard the day of his death as my day of jubilee should give you an idea as to the depth of my matrimonial misery. I can't deny that I was relieved when the marriage was over.

## I Want It All

What came next was even more unexpected. As soon as David heard that Nabal was gone, he proposed marriage. Oh, if I had known how precisely the prayers of several nights before would be answered, I might have felt a twinge of guilt in praying them. Here I was, free of Nabal, preparing to marry David. All five of my attending maidens were chattering with excitement as we prepared to go. I was in heaven.

David was every bit the husband I had longed for. He had that rare combination of manliness and sensitivity that captures, then melts, a woman. I went from asking God, "What did I do to deserve such misery?" to "What did I do to deserve such bliss?" I had a time of euphoria, a period of walking on air, into which came only one nagging negativity—the nearly unconscious belief that something just *had* to go wrong. This was, of course, accompanied by the hope that nothing would. But it did.

"Abigail, this is Ahinoam," David said soon after our wedding night. Before me stood a lovely woman, roughly my age, with the same type of smile upon her lips that I was forcing. I had worried about sharing David with Michal, Saul's daughter, but then heard she had been given to another man. The thought of David actually taking *another* wife never even crossed my naive mind. Well, naive no more; here she was.

Regardless of how comfortable our culture was with polygamy, I never found it to be comfortable, and I think I can speak for most wives and concubines. The feminine heart wants two things of love: honesty and exclusiveness. I had the first— David honestly loved me. The trouble was, he honestly loved another as well. And another, and another, and another . . .

Shortly after our wedding Saul perished by his own sword, and David took the throne. Seven years later he won the civil war between Israel and Judah and became king over both. By this time David had four additional wives . . . and counting. A few more years passed, and in spite of his growing harem, David committed adultery with Bathsheba and had her husband murdered. It was at that point that I realized that David's proclivity for acquiring the affections of women didn't spring so much from his desire to build the royal family as it did from a love addiction that he couldn't seem to master. David was extravagantly gifted in the art of courtship, and he couldn't seem to resist exercising his gift whenever the opportunity presented itself. The result was that I never had him to myself, except in the delirious moments behind bedroom curtains, and they were fleeting.

As I mentioned, I had two disappointments in love: Nabal because he was incapable of love, and David because he was so good at it that I was forced to share him with others. Surprisingly, though, I have peace. I have had the best and the worst that romance can offer, and it's as fickle as a desert wind. It blows one way, then another; it wafts in the sweet breath of balsam; it throws sand in your face. God answered my prayer for love, gave me the best this world had to offer, and still it wasn't enough. I touch the Hand that brought me the gift and I trace it back, back to the Giver. I hold the hand of that Giver and rest content in His love, which never fails.

*(Get the story of Abigail and David for yourself in 1 Samuel 25:2-44;*
*2 Samuel 3:1-5; 5:12, 13; 11:1-22.)*

## COGITATIONS

1. Why do you think God allowed polygamy in Old Testament times? Are there modern forms of polygamy?

2. Is it possible to have true intimacy in a marriage when love is not exclusive?

3. Is lifelong romance possible? Why is it so rare?

# Lions, Boars, and Floating Doors

here was once a man named Admetus who loved a beautiful woman named Alcestis.

The father of the beauty proclaimed one day that he would give his daughter's hand in marriage to whichever young man came to fetch her in a chariot drawn by lions and boars. Now, lion-and-boar-drawn chariots were not easy to come by in those days, and so the father was essentially saying that his daughter was unattainable. Little did he realize, though, that her admirer, Admetus, had the god Apollo at his command, for Apollo was being punished by the gods, and his punishment was working for a mortal for a given period of time. Apollo, being a god, had no trouble conjuring up a lion-and-boar drawn chariot for Admetus. The amazed father had no choice but to surrender his lovely girl to the man in the big-pig-and-killer-cat mobile. At last Alcestis belonged to the man who loved her.

But tragedy struck. Admetus, before the relationship could even be enjoyed, discovered that he was terminally ill. The future looked grim until again the gods interposed, telling Admetus that he would live if he found someone to die in his place.

Admetus began a desperate search for just such a person. First he approached his servants, but they refused. Next he propositioned his aged parents, whom he reasoned had little left of their lives anyway, but they also declined. (Can you imagine? "Hey, Mom, wanna take my death sentence?") Many attempts later Admetus despaired completely of finding someone to die for him.

Then a volunteer was found. Admetus could live! Oh, how the man rejoiced that he would be allowed to enjoy his bride . . . until he discovered that it was his bride, Alcestis, who had volunteered to die for him. As much as they pitied the man who would lose her, *the onlookers stood in awe of the nobility of the woman willing to give herself for the one she loved.*

This ancient Greek myth depicts the depths of human love. Sometimes—*rarely*, but sometimes—a human will love another human so much that they will be willing to die in their place. The person that provokes such love is always exceptional—exceptionally beautiful, noble, gifted, or good. Admetus, in the mind of his bride, was good enough to be worthy of dying love.

The highest expression of human love is to die for a good person. God's love did more—it died for *bad* people. The myth of Alcestis and Admetus is probably what inspired the following well-known passage:

"For one will hardly die for a righteous man; though perhaps for the good man someone would dare even to die. But God demonstrates His own love toward us, in that while we were yet sinners, Christ died for us" (Romans 5:7, 8, NASB).

The romance of Jack and Rose in the movie *Titanic* was similar to the love of Admetus and Alcestis—except this time the man died for the woman. When Jack tried to climb aboard the fragment of door that Rose floated upon, it became clear that it would tip over, and they would both fall into the icy waters. Only one of them could be saved. Resigning himself to death, Jack said, "Never let go, Rose; never let go," and sunk to his grave. She was so good, so beautiful, so worth dying for that he willingly let her live instead of himself.

Touching, but human love at its big-screen best falls short of God's love. If *Titanic* had tried to depict the love of God, Jack's worst enemy would be floating on the door, cursing and swearing and spewing out insults. He would smell like a dead rat. He would have a hideous face and a deformed body. Still, Jack would love his enemy enough to surrender to death that he might live—not to immortalize the ugliness, but to give his enemy a chance to become something better. Such is the nature of God's love.

"While we were enemies we were reconciled to God through the death of His Son" (Romans 5:10, NASB).

The greatest love in the world is not the love of something beautiful and virtuous, but the love of something ugly and sinful. You can't find this love anywhere in this world, but you can find it in God's Word. It doesn't sell many movies, but it does buy an eternity of joy. Buy it, or rather let it buy you, and you will never want a refund.

## TRY IT OUT

1. Read the chapter "Gethsemane" in *The Desire of Ages.* Write a poem based on the chapter that answers the question: What is God's love like?

2. Send your poem to a youth publication such as *Insight,* or photocopy it and share it with friends and acquaintances.

3. Is there anyone you consider to be your enemy? Think of which person that might be, then follow the advice of the Proverbs—*literally:* "If your enemy is hungry, give him food to eat; and if he is thirsty, give him water to drink" (Proverbs 25:21, NASB). A small token of food—a bag of chips or a sweet—should shock that person's socks off.

4. "Love your enemies, and pray for those who persecute you" (Matthew 5:44, NASB). This is the advice of Jesus. Do you pray for people who do you wrong? Try it; you'll like it!

## CROSS-EXAMINE THE WITNESS

 *Our witness is Gabe Kramer, a student at Southwestern Adventist University in Keene, Texas. A senior journalism major, he loves writing, photography, and spending time with friends. He also loves to make others laugh, even at his own expense.*

QUESTION: WHAT PART CAN ROMANCE PLAY IN THE LIFE OF A CHRISTIAN?

A t least once a week we bow our heads in reverence, asking God to make us servants, show us His will, and guide us closer to Him. God takes our pleas seriously. God showed me one of my biggest hindrances from a closer walk with Him—my insistence on dating before His appointed time. The problem? I sought a relationship for comfort and complete fulfillment instead of searching for that in Christ. He told me I needed to trust Him with this dating business. That meant to stop looking for it. To seek first His kingdom and how to serve others. "For even the Son of Man did not come to be served, but to serve, and to give His life a ransom for many" (Mark 10:45, NASB).

There was this girl who sang in a gospel choir at my school. I knew she was spiritual and loved the Lord with all her heart. That attracted me so much! I found myself looking for her, wanting to talk with her, and thinking about her. A *lot*.

But it wasn't His time. How did I know? Because I hadn't made Him the love of my life first. Conclusion: I stopped trying to force situations for togetherness. That protected her heart from being led on, and I'll never regret doing that. How do I know she isn't the one? I don't. But His will was carried out.

Do you want to follow God? Deny yourself (Matthew 16:24), and He will give you the desires of your heart (Psalm 37:4), in His time.

Oh, and He gives joy, too.

# The Levite's Concubine's Father

*"In those days there was no king in Israel; every man did what was right in his own eyes."*

JUDGES 17:6, NASB.

She was always such a passionate girl, fighting her way through everything. It didn't surprise me when she showed up at my doorstep in tears, saying that she and her man weren't getting along. I knew he probably missed her terribly, as she was one of those women you couldn't live with or without. I felt for the poor man—she had a way of locking onto your heart like the ring in a slave's nose, both painfully and permanently. Ah, my daughter, I loved her.

Her man came crawling, of course. I was thrilled to see him, praying and hoping for reconciliation. I have to admit that, in spite my awareness of my daughter's charms, I never expected her to land a man of such, shall we say, stature. Priests did not traditionally have concubines, but then Israel had slid into apostasy and nothing seemed to matter anymore. Consequently, I had a daughter living in sin with a holy man.

The Levite spoke tenderly to the girl, hoping she would return home with him in time. Fortunately, he was in no rush to leave, so while he milked out the wooing process for all it was worth, we had time to enjoy each other's company. I found him to be an affable man, not particularly spiritual, but a good comrade. We put the very best on the table for him—everything from freshly roasted goat to salty olives to sweet, fleshy figs. And I admit the two of us consumed our fair share of wine those first three days.

On the fourth morning of his stay they both came announcing their departure.

"Have something to eat first," I urged. Sincerely thinking that it would be a quick breakfast, they sat down, only to begin again with the social festivities. It was truly amazing how the two of us men found so much to talk about, from the price of barley to the local Levite gossip. We shot back and forth with our opinions, gradually acquiring that sense of power that comes when you solve the world's problems in the course of a conversation.

Time passed by unnoticed while the sun made a full arc over the land, and when it at last began to sink into the west, I said, "You can't leave now. Stay until tomorrow." And they did.

The next day was the same routine. I got them to eat before they left, not just a quick bite but the usually multi-course feast. This lasted into the afternoon, when the priest made his usual announcement of departure, and I made my usual plea for them to stay. This time it didn't work. With less than a few hours of traveling time left, the Levite and my daughter set out with their entourage of two donkeys and a servant.

I should have pleaded harder. I knew it wasn't ideal for them to leave at that late hour. How many times I've wished I had summoned all my considerable powers of persuasion to get them to stay the night, then sent them off early the next day. Oh, the rewriting of history that goes on in the mind once tragedy strikes.

The Levite himself informed me of the events of the night in Gibeah, and I'm amazed that he had the courage to tell me. He made it a point to stay in an Israelite city. Right around sunset they rolled into Gibeah, a city of the tribe of Benjamin. *Here is a place,* the priest thought, *we will be safe.* I would have thought the same thing.

When they entered the town square, people were milling

about them, most of them preparing to head home after a day's work or shopping. The travelers sat and waited for the usual invitation to dinner and lodging, but none came. This should have been their first sign that all was not as it should have been in this city of Benjamin. God's people should be the friendliest, most hospitable people on earth! When the well of common courtesy dries up, you can pretty well assume that the source spring of moral decency has long ceased to flow as well. In other words, rude people are probably bad people.

Finally an old man, not even a resident of Gibeah, but a migrant farmer from Ephraim, saw them sitting forlornly and struck up a conversation. The Ephraimite invited them all back to his house and fed them from his own pantry, washing their feet, taking care of their animals, the whole nine yards. It seemed as if the evening would be pleasantly uneventful.

Then dinner was interrupted by a pounding upon the door, followed by bellowing voices. A shout was heard, "Bring out the man who came into your house, that we may have relations with him!" Low-life perverts, a whole crowd of them, surrounded the little house, demanding that the priest become their sexual toy for the night.

The old Ephraimite stepped outside. I suppose I should congratulate him for his bravery, but I have a hard time doing that in the light of what followed. He said, "No, fellows, please do not act so wickedly! Here, I have a virgin daughter, and my guest has a concubine! Take them and do whatever you want to them, but don't take the man!" He was defending the priest, yes, but offering up his own daughter and mine as scapegoats.

Where did we get this idea that the value of human beings can be quantified like the value of a vineyard or a cow? The strong ones, the ones that make the money, are considered more valuable, and the dependent ones, the ones that aren't allowed to make money, are expendable. Newborn baby boys call forth a neighborhood feast, while baby girls are taken quietly to the dunghill and left there to die. The strong are sacrificed *for;* the weak are sacrificed. This is always the way it is when God is absent, from a society or an individual heart.

The perverts continued to demand the priest. No doubt the fellow was desperate to protect himself from violation, knowing that the men outside would find a way to break into the house if they were not placated somehow. In a mindless moment, a moment when he had to have forgotten my daughter's love, my hospitality, and God's grace all at once, he seized her and brought her out to them. The page is stained with my tears as I think about what happened next. I can't even bring myself to write it down.

Sunrise, mockingly cheerful sunrise, came that day as any other. The sun rises on the just and on the unjust, on the abused and on the abuser. My daughter dragged herself, tenacious little thing that she was, to the door of the house, where the priest found her after having a good night's sleep. Her hands were wrapped upon the threshold of the door like a suppliant seeking mercy. How strange, when she should have been seeking justice.

"Get up; let's go," the priest said. There was no answer, because my little girl was dead.

He placed her dead body upon his donkey and set out for home in Ephraim. Upon arriving home, he decided upon a course of action that would jerk Israel to its senses in regard to its moral condition. Whether he was motivated by pity for himself or my daughter, I don't know. Yes, she had been raped to death, but he had lost a piece of property, hadn't he? I'm sorry if sarcasm is getting the better of me.

He broke her dead body into 12 pieces—a calf here, a forearm there . . . I wouldn't doubt it if he sent the head itself to Benjamin. If I have lost respect for him, I have retained respect for his cleverness. He sent out the accusation of a crime and its proof all in the same package. An innocent girl was murdered in a city of Benjamin—here is a hunk of her corpse to prove it. Any doubters?

The scheme succeeded in arousing the sensibilities of the nation. Civil war followed, and after a grisly battle Benjamin was nearly wiped off the face of the earth. But that is not my concern. My concern, in my daughter's absence, is for all the daughters who are left. I can't help asking myself, *How could I have made her*

*safer?* I could have started by teaching her as a child not to trust herself with men who did not respect her. The Levite's act of surrendering my daughter was not an isolated mistake on his part, but a manifestation of just how self-centered his "love" really was. He showed this self-centeredness first by being willing to take from her what should belong only to a husband. He wanted, like so many men, the perks of marriage without the obligations of it. This fatal flaw in their relationship needed only to meet the ultimate test to become obvious. He didn't love her; he used her to love himself. And when it came down to himself and her, he chose himself. It wasn't a departure from his character; it was a magnification of it.

The character of the society was just as bad. Any society that places a lower estimate upon women merely because they are weaker physically and politically will eventually start to kill off its babies and old people. But remember that this mind-set was there because the culture had *strayed* from God, not because it had followed Him. God always seems to get the black eye that people deserve. If God had been present, my daughter would have been safe. After all, He is the great Father of all daughters, and His tears stain not just this page but every page of history upon which a girl is harmed.

*"The Lord will guard your going out and your coming in from this time forth and forever."*

PSALM 121:8, NASB.

*(Get the story for yourself of the Levite, his concubine, and her father in Judges 19.)*

## COGITATIONS

1. Why was there such a low estimate placed upon the value of women during the time of the judges? Are there examples of Bible characters who deeply respected women?

2. When a society places a low estimate upon women, it usually

does the same to children, the unborn, the elderly. Why is this?

3. While rape, abuse, and violence are not the fault of the victim, are there some things we can do to lessen the chances that something like that will happen to us? If so, what?

# The Locket

*"Do not fear those who kill the body, but are unable to kill the soul; but rather fear Him who is able to destroy both soul and body in hell."*

MATTHEW 10:28, NASB.

 t was in a land called Ruination that the locket was first given. An ambassador from the healing fields came to the people of Ruination with a basket filled with the golden treasures. Day and night he cried out in the city streets, offering his priceless wares for free. "Take your locket! Take your free locket! It will preserve your soul from the effects of this cursed land! It will ensure you an entrance into the healing fields."

Many ignored the ambassador, and some showed mild interest. A few approached with questions, such as "Will I become rich? Will I be cured of all disease? Will my house become safe from thieves?"

To these questions the ambassador would honestly reply, "No, it will neither increase your fortunes nor remove your difficulties in this land. It *will* keep you from adding to your own sorrows, though, and it will ensure your safety in the healing fields at last, when the land of Ruination comes to an end. Oh, take a locket; *take a locket!*"

"What does the locket contain?" a wide-eyed child asked.

The ambassador eagerly replied, "It contains a drop of the life essence of the great Prince of the healing fields. This is the most precious substance that can be found anywhere under the sun. It is more precious than any amount of good things this land can give you. The Prince gave it at infinite cost to Himself but as a free gift to you. Please, please, *take a locket!*"

Finally a few of the citizens of Ruination edged toward the ambassador with upturned hands. From above, it was a pathetic sight to see. Droves of people darted about, many crippled or ill, dressed in dark, filthy clothing, ignoring the ambassador, while a few ragged ones, mostly children, crept toward him. Into each willing hand he would place a golden locket, which would gleam bright against their grubby fingers. The locket would then be hung around their necks, and they would wander off, some to tell others about the locket-bearer and others not to.

A week after the ambassador had arrived in Ruination, the dawn brought a band of angry men to the place where he cried out in the street.

"Some of the ones to whom you gave the locket," they snarled, "have met with misfortune. Diseases. Crimes. Even death! The locket did them no good!"

A muscular, dirty man walked forward holding the pale, limp body of a child. There, tossed among the rags she wore, was the gleaming golden locket. "My daughter took one of your lockets!" he cried. "It did not help her! She died of the plague last night in her sleep!"

A frail-looking old woman limped forward with a locket in her hand. "I took one of your lockets, and I was attacked and beaten by thieves!" she cried.

A young mother with streaming tears took the ambassador by his collar, sobbing, "All three of my children took one of your lockets, and all three of them were kidnapped last night!"

The ambassador composed himself and spoke softly. "Certainly the locket is not to blame. Would not these things have happened anyway in this land of Ruination?"

This question was met with silence. The people knew that their land had always been filled with these terrors.

"Yet for those who gladly receive the locket," the ambassador said, "there is a safety that transcends the misfortunes of life in Ruination. Those who die with the locket will partake of that life-essence given so freely to them by the prince of the healing fields, and they will live at last in a place far more worthy of them than this desperate land!"

"How can we know?" the muscular man shouted.

"You must believe," said the ambassador. "Certainly the prince of the healing fields would not leave the people of this land without an escape, for he gave up his very life-essence in order to provide that escape."

One by one the scorners departed from the ambassador, who took up with his task, calling out to passersby, "Please, take a locket! Take a free locket! You will live forever in the healing fields! Please, *take a locket!*" As he continued to cry out day after day, he heard the scoffing of doubters, felt the sailing stones of haters, and saw the cold, heartless backs of unbelief. The ambassador marveled that the people of Ruination would refuse the hope of life in the healing fields merely because they were not assured of immediate prosperity and perfect safety. Yet to this day he continues to call out, day after day, week after week, year after year, offering his treasures to all who will take them.

*"These things I have spoken to you, that in Me you may have peace. In the world you have tribulation, but take courage; I have overcome the world."*

JOHN 16:33, NASB.

## TRY IT OUT

1. Divide a paper into two columns. On one side, write "sufferers"; on the other, "ultimate good." Look for biblical examples of people who suffered and give details about *how* they suffered. Across from each entry write down what ultimate good came

from their suffering. (Hint: A good person to start with is Job.)

2. Write out the following promises on index cards, and keep them with you to meditate on whenever you feel unsafe: Isaiah 43:1, 2; Psalm 3:1-4; Matthew 11:28-30.

## CROSS-EXAMINE THE WITNESS

*Our witness wishes to remain anonymous.*

QUESTION: GOD HATES TO SEE PEOPLE HURT AND ABUSE ONE ANOTHER, BUT SOMETIMES HE ALLOWS IT. WHAT CAN WE LEARN FROM THIS TERRIBLE EXPERIENCE?

When I was in fifth grade, a group of kids banded together and attacked me on the playground at school. At the time I couldn't make sense of what happened, but now I realize that God can actually bring a blessing from the curse. Because of this experience I can relate to what Jesus experienced at the Crucifixion. My heart is drawn close to Him in suffering because of what I suffered.

No, I would never have chosen this experience, and I hope I never have to go through it again. I wouldn't wish it on anyone! But I do see the light at the end of the tunnel.

# Security

# The Frightened Young Men

*"We will know by this that we are of the truth, and will assure our heart before Him, in whatever our heart condemns us; for God is greater than our heart, and knows all things."*

1 JOHN 3:19, 20, NASB.

felt in my teenage soul that I had seen it all—lepers cleansed, devils cast out, people speaking in tongues, you name it. This was the time of the rain of God's Spirit, the afterglow of the great Pentecost. Both miracles and disasters were popping up on every side, and I was enjoying every minute of the wild ride.

The high of highs came when a group of us were at our house one night having a spontaneous prayer meeting. First on the prayer list was the fact that Peter was in prison. James had been killed by the sword at Herod's command, and we pleaded that Peter would not meet the same fate.

A knock came on the door. We sent our servant Rhoda to answer it because we were too busy praying.

"O God in heaven," someone was pleading, "if it be Thy will, see to it that Peter is delivered—"

"Peter is standing at the front gate!" A voice cut through the prayers. Reluctantly eyes opened and searched the room to find the source of the rude interruption. It was Rhoda. She continued, her face lit, her voice ringing out so shrill that my eardrums rattled, insisting in the face of skeptics that it was true, really true.

"You're crazy!"

"No, no!" she continued her hyper-excited announcement.

"It's his angel, then!" someone said, followed by a near-silence with only a faint *knock, knock, knock* coming from the front gate. There was a bit of a mass migration for the gate at that moment, and when it opened, Peter walked in.

Wow. I could hardly grasp it. The people prayed, and God answered. So quickly, in fact, that even the ones who prayed were caught off guard. This Christianity was powerful stuff!

Looking back, though, I think I was a little too infatuated with the *power*. The real core of Christianity is love, and the power just sort of grows out of that. I don't think I got the love part at the beginning of my experience, because as John always said, "perfect love casts out fear" (1 John 4:18, NASB), and I had loads of fear. The fact that I was overcome with *fear* betrayed my lack of *love*. I am known by many as a coward now. My ego is not happy with this, but at least I can help people overcome their own fear by relating how I overcame mine. After all, you can't overcome fear if you're afraid of fear itself. So I will share with you how perfect love casts out fear, even the fear of *fear*, which I am no longer afraid of.

The great apostle Paul would visit our house from time to time. Mom was a wealthy woman, and we had plenty of extra space for Paul and his friends, whomever they happened to be. This time he came with Barnabas, who is my cousin and a great man. The two of them were sharing some of their ministry stories with my mom when the hair started standing up on the back of my neck. I began to sense that God was calling me to join them.

"Can I come with you on your next trip?" I asked, sort of blurting out the question. Paul was reserved and dignified, but cousin Barnabas smiled warmly. The two looked me up and down for a moment.

"I . . . feel God's favor in my heart . . . and I just want to be totally *His,*" I said. They continued to stare as if through a veil, the way someone looks at you and doesn't see you because they are really thinking of something else. Since then I have understood that they were just praying silently. Evidently God gave them the go-ahead, because very soon after we were packing up to leave.

First stop: the island of Cyprus. I was really psyched. To be with those two great minds, to watch them in action, to see them battle with demons in human form, and to hear them preach the gospel—this was what I loved about ministry. The high point was our encounter with Bar-Jesus. I know, what a weird name. It means "son of Jesus," but I guarantee there was no relationship whatsoever to Jesus Christ. He was a Jewish sorcerer in the city of Paphos, a false prophet, and just like the false prophets of ancient Israel he was a real nut case. The deputy of Cyprus wanted to hear the gospel message, but this citizen of hell filled the deputy's head with all kinds of confusion before Paul could get to him. Paul dealt with the situation like a soldier on the march, seeking out the magic man so they could talk eyeball to eyeball. He didn't bother with chitchat:

"You liar! You cheat! You son of the devil! You enemy of righteousness! Are you going to keep making straight roads crooked? God is going to deal with you now! He is going to strike you with blindness!"

Sure enough, Mr. Self-appointed Prophet instantly began to grope for a hand to hold, staring into space. This had the effect of affirming the message that Paul and Barnabas preached, and the deputy ate it all up after that. What a victory! I felt as good as when I won our neighborhood arm-wrestling playoffs.

But then things went downhill. We set sail for a city called Perga, and the sailing conditions were rough. The days that followed are a blur, but I recall the lack of hospitality that I thought we would always have. I also recall lack of funds to buy the simple things we needed, such as lodging and food. I recall tossing all night on the cold ground, unable to stop shivering, listening to my stomach moan.

I asked Barnabas one day how the future looked.

"To be honest, not good," he said. "In fact, things may get a little tougher before they get easier."

I panicked. I didn't see how things could *get* any worse! Acting purely out of fear, I said, "Then I'm going home to Mom."

Barnabas didn't try to stop me. He even tried to give me a vision for future missionary journeys, but I wasn't thinking about my calling as a Christian—I was thinking about Mom's home-made bread and the warm fire of our hearth. I'm still a little embarrassed to say it, but I deserted the cause of God.

Once I got home, the bread didn't taste so good and the fire wasn't so warm. Mom's kisses weren't even as sweet as they once were, because my life was soured by failure. I was like a fox forced by my fear to live in a dark hole, and every bite of food and ray of sunshine felt as if it were stolen, just as a fox creeps out and snatches quail from the neighbor's yard. Fear—which is essentially looking out for yourself—had made a slave out of me, and I hated my life.

Months later Paul and Barnabas were in Antioch. They had been to many cities in that region: Iconium, Lystra, Derbe, and up to Pisidian Antioch. I would hear about their adventures from time to time, but the news would only pierce my soul. It was so hard to be sad while everyone else was joyful, and what was worse, I was sad about them doing great things for God! It wasn't that I didn't want them to succeed; it's just that I knew that *I* could have been there if I had been more brave. That voice, the same type of voice that the Bar-Jesus guy had, would hiss in my ear every time a mission report came in: "You could've been there, but you ran scared! You're a coward, John Mark, a real noodle in the wind. You'll never amount to anything!" I couldn't fight the conviction that the voice was speaking truth, and my heart just caved in like a sand house washed by a wave.

Then one day Barnabas showed up at our door. Barnabas, silver-haired, twinkle-eyed Barnabas. I could see why the Lyconians called him Zeus—he always wore this kind smile, and he sort of glowed like Moses coming down from Sinai. I would have been terrified to see him, but that warm smile just melted away my fear.

"Barnabas, I am such a loser!" I broke down. "I can't even look at myself in the glass . . . I'm a coward, aren't I?" Somehow I could ask Barnabas that question and actually want an answer.

"We're all cowards," he said putting his hands on my shoulders.

"No, no, not you," I said.

"Yes, me," he said, "but something greater than fear has taken possession of my life. The more I understand the love of God, the less I worry about myself. It's not me that drives me; it's God's Spirit. Do you want that experience again, young man?"

The familiar hair-prickling-on-my-neck feeling came back, only this time all up and down my back.

"Yes, but it's too—"

"Will you come with me?" he cut me off in midlament. There it was again, the invitation. Barnabas had returned several days' journey to Jerusalem, not just to inform the saints and refresh his body, but to get *me*. Me! The insecure mama's boy! The deserter! The no-account has-been. God wasn't done with me after all!

And so it was that the love of God through Barnabas washed away my fear. I saw in my cousin this Jesus whose glory and goodness drove him right through painful obstacles, like a battering ram pushed through a wooden door. I learned later that Paul and Barnabas had parted ways over the issue of whether I could still be used in ministry or not. Paul said no; Barnabas said yes. I respect Paul, and since then we have become good friends, but it was Barnabas who made the difference of life and death for me. I was infatuated with power, rendered powerless by fear, then empowered by love. This time it's for real.

*(Get the story of John Mark for yourself in Acts 12:12-25; 13:5-13; 15:37-41;*
The Acts of the Apostles, *pages 166, 167, and 202.)*

# The Young Man With the Linen Sheet

*"There is no fear in love; but perfect love casts out fear, because fear involves punishment, and the one who fears is not perfected in love. We love, because He first loved us."*

1 JOHN 4: 18, 19, NASB.

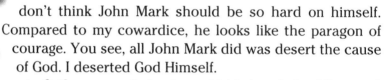

don't think John Mark should be so hard on himself. Compared to my cowardice, he looks like the paragon of courage. You see, all John Mark did was desert the cause of God. I deserted God Himself.

It was in Gethsemane. Judas brought his band of soldiers and thugs to the garden, where they found Jesus after His prayer. It was so ridiculous how they came with swords and clubs, as if Jesus were some savage beast that was going to tear them limb from limb. There they stood, breathing hard, sweating, ready for combat . . . and then there He was, calm and gentle as always. The religious power figures en masse pitted against the weaponless wanderer and His fishermen followers—what a mockery.

"Rabbi!" The words exuded Judas's lips like scented vapor, deadly sweet. A kiss was planted on the cheek that would soon be covered with spit and shredded with thorns.

"Judas," the Lord still spoke with love, "are you betraying the Son of man with a kiss?" Couldn't he have done it with a kick or a shove or a slap? Why did he have to defile the universal symbol of affection with his hypocrisy?

"Whom are you looking for?" Jesus cried to the looming crowd.

"Jesus of Nazareth!"

"Here I am. Let the others go," He said.

Let the others go. Let them escape even the grazing of the sword that would cut Him into ribbons. How could anyone be so selfless as to let His friends leave? How could those friends be so *selfish* as to actually do it? These questions still haunt me.

The next thing I remember is Peter's hacking off the ear of the high priest's slave. Great, Peter, that's what we need—more negative PR. But no problem—Jesus, gentle Jesus, willing-to-die-rather-than-sin Jesus, put the ear right back on as if the man were an assembled toy.

"Stop! No more of this!" He reckoned with His impulsive friend. "Do you think that I can't request that My Father send Me thousands of angels? All this is necessary for Scripture to be fulfilled. Let it happen."

Let it happen? The reality began to dawn on Peter that Jesus was going to *let* His enemies do their murder thing. That's when Petros the rock shifted like the sand and blew away, along with the dithering disciples. They all forsook Him and fled. Away. Into the cold, sad night where ninnies hide behind bushes rather than stand up for God.

As for me, I felt goose bumps on my skin, chilled and damp under the linen sheet I was wearing. It was my only garment, and the only thing between me and the ravaging beasts. Could I stick close to the friend who stuck closer than a brother? I looked at His face, all holy and childlike. He was alone. I felt the pull of fidelity, of faith. I wanted to be there for Him, but just at the moment my mind was reaching a point of decision, I caught the face of one of the thugs in the mob. Animal, not human, wanting a feast of innocent blood before he slept. Then a shout came, and the thug, along with several others in the crowd, lunged at me.

Hands with strong, digging fingers grabbed my arms. Somehow wrenching free, I twirled away from them, and because they were holding my linen sheet, I twirled out of my clothes as well, running off buck naked into the night.

Naked. That's what you are without God. If you let fear propel you into the darkness, you will find yourself shivering in the bushes, hoping someone will lend you a garment until you can earn the money to buy another for yourself.

I'm sure you're wondering how things turned out for me, but

I'm going to let you wonder. As far as my spiritual state was concerned, I did find cover. No, no one lent me a garment, but Jesus gave me one. This is the amazing part of my story. Fear led me to run from my God, who was my only righteousness. Once I ran from my righteousness, I found myself as naked as the poorest beggar. While I hid, Jesus was striped naked and exposed to the world on my behalf. He took the nakedness that was mine so that He could give me His own righteousness to wear.

I believe God has a sense of humor, and I believe He communicates to us through the experiences of life. I see in my experience of being shucked out of my shorts an analogy of my spiritual journey. First, fear led to flight. Flight brought nakedness, and with it even more fear. Then, even as I quivered and quaked, Christ died to clothe me, and in so doing, freed me from the bondage of fear. Why don't you learn from my mistake instead of having to make your own, and receive His righteousness right now before fear drives you to do something crazy, such as abandon your best friend and your clothes at the same time?

*(Get the story of the young man with the linen sheet for yourself from Mark 14:51, 52.)*

## COGITATIONS

1. Rewrite these powerful thoughts from Hebrews 2:14, 15 in your own words: "Since then the children share in flesh and blood, He Himself likewise also partook of the same, that through death He might render powerless him who had the power of death, that is, the devil, and might free those who through fear of death were subject to slavery all their lives" (NASB).

2. Why does the ultimate fear, the fear of death, make us "subject to slavery"? Since fear makes slaves out of us, what does security do?

3. Does God want us to have security in Him? If so, which of the

following should that security be based on: a knowledge of His character of perfect love or a knowledge that we have obeyed Him? Both? Something else?

# Juniper Meets the Giant

*"It is He who sits above the circle of the earth, and its inhabitants are like grasshoppers."*

ISAIAH 40:22, NASB.

One day long ago, through some strange twist of the supernatural, a young girl named Juniper found herself lost in the land of a race of giants called the Gargantuans. As she crept down the wooded path, she could hear their booming voices in the distance, and several times she spotted them in the valley below when the path took a turn to the top of a precipice. At one such precipice Juniper settled her tired body into the base of a huge banyan tree, observing the Gargantuans below from her hiding place behind the smaller trunks of the tree. Most of the mammoths seemed bent upon evil of some sort, hunching their shoulders and alternating between loud ranting and sardonic snickers. Oh, what would she do if discovered by a giant? The smoke of their fires rose to tickle her tiny nostrils and make the behemoths seem all the nearer. In spite of her fear, though, Juniper could not fight sleep indefinitely, and soon she sailed off into oblivion.

When the morning sun arose, Juniper's eyes fluttered open to a sight that sent a shock wave up her small spine. There before her, blinking almost as fast as her own eyes, was a pair of eyes so large that Juniper could have crawled completely into a tear duct. The lower half of the face was hidden by the cliff, behind which the beast was standing, exposing only his upper face and a crop of unruly white hair. The individual strands of hair on the head and in the eyebrows were so thick that Juniper, if she had dared to pluck one, could have tied it like a rope around her waist and used it for any number of utilitarian functions. The beast was so huge, so powerful, and the girl so small that all that stood between her and death was the character and intentions of the monster. In terms of Juniper's destiny, everything hinged upon the giant's heart.

"Are you . . . going to kill me?" Juniper whispered. With that, the head, of which she saw only half, tipped itself to the side, resembling in largeness of motion the swaying of a giant house in a tornado. The huge eyes then took on a look of supreme puzzlement, in which Juniper thought she might have detected a flicker of pity. The giant seemed confused.

"You're a giant! I'm—I'm little! *What are you going to do with me?*" the girl shouted now, her internal hysteria finally fighting its way into sound.

With this the head levitated, because, in fact, the giant stood up straighter to expose his entire face to the girl. He cleared his throat, which sounded and felt roughly like a thunderstorm, and began to speak, projecting such a wind that the girl was nearly pinned to the tree.

"I—I won't hurt you."

The teeth of the Gargantuan, peering out from behind huge lips, were adequate to sever Juniper in one swift bite. Somehow, though, the girl's fear was abating as she watched the giant's face. At this moment a huge hand lowered itself to the ground in front of the banyan tree, where Juniper was still somewhat shielded by the small trunks that circled the base like a fence. The palm of the giant's hand was upturned, as if to bid her entrance.

Now, Juniper knew that she had only two choices. She could try to escape, or she could walk right into the hand that could crush her. If the giant was truly good, she would live either way; if evil, she would *die* either way. The final factor in her decision was that of potential friendship. If she succumbed to the giant's invitation, she could, perhaps, find him to be as kind and good as he was huge. If she ran, she would never know, unless he killed her, in which case she would be dead. She had a friend to gain, and nothing at all to lose, and so after these calculations were confirmed in her thinking, she stepped out from her prison of banyan trunks into the giant's upturned hand.

You may want to know the outcome of this girl's venture into the unknown, in which case you will have to delve into the archives of your own imaginings. Let it be said, though, that the dynamics of the giant and the girl are oh-so-similar to the relation between the soul and God. In a dangerous land where all seem untrustworthy, we encounter a Being so powerful that He could be our undoing or our salvation. Based on the goodness we think we see, the evidence of His Word, we venture into His hand, hoping for the best. In the end our decision to stay in that hand is based on who He proves Himself to be, again and again. There is a risk involved in finding security in God! There is also a risk involved in fleeing from it. Which risk will you take? From experience with the Giant Himself, I recommend the former.

## TRY IT OUT

1. Is there a young child in your life? Ask them if they would like you to read them a story. Then when they say yes, which they probably will, tell the story of Baby Moses in your own words (Exodus 2:1-10). Give them a pad and paper and let them draw what they hear. Discuss what it means to have God care for you the way He did for Moses.

2. Most conceited people are horribly insecure. Think of someone who is typically self-inflated, and instead of putting them in their place, assure them that you are their friend. Make sure not to use flattery, which will only make things worse, but rather encouragement.

## CROSS-EXAMINE THE WITNESS

*Our witness is Shawn Brace, a student at Andrews University in Michigan. Shawn writes and sings his own songs. He is such a good role model that some friends named their baby after him.*

QUESTION: WHAT IS THE DIFFERENCE BETWEEN THE SECURITY THE WORLD OFFERS AND WHAT GOD OFFERS US IN CHRIST?

Have you ever lost a set of keys? Maybe you've misplaced them somewhere and forgotten where you've left them, or maybe they just dropped out of your pocket, or maybe someone stole them. Losing your keys is one of the worst feelings in the world. I should know—last year I lost my keys somewhere on my school campus and couldn't find them. I searched and searched, but my efforts were for nothing. I didn't drive my car for about three weeks afterward because I didn't have another key. I finally had a new key made for my car—but had to pay a pretty penny. It was an awful feeling to know that someone could have full access to my car, my room, and wherever else my keys would get them.

We all have our ideas of security. We see commercials on TV all the time about security systems—"we're home, even when you're not." We find comfort in knowing that a bunch of bolts on our door will keep us safe from intruders. But if someone really wanted to get into our houses, would bolts prevent them?

Others of us find security in the arms of our boyfriends or girlfriends. We don't feel complete unless we are with them. But what happens when they break up with us? There is only one true meaning of security—being in the arms of Jesus. Through all the struggles and trials and disappointments in life, Jesus is there. Although physically you may be beat up, it's encouraging to know that Jesus will "never leave you nor forsake you" (Hebrews 13:5, NKJV). What a comforting thought!

# Self-worth

# Mephibosheth

*"I called upon thy name, O Lord, out of the low dungeon. Thou hast heard my voice: hide not thine ear at my breathing, at my cry."*

LAMENTATIONS 3:55, 56.

I am Mephibosheth—"he who scatters shame." Does my name mean that I send shame away, shattered into unrecognizable pieces? Or does it mean that I throw handfuls of it to the wind, the way a sower scatters seed, that it might bring forth more devastation? I will let you decide after you hear my story, beginning (when I was 5 years old) with the most calamitous event of my life.

## THE FALL

My nanny burst through the door, moving much more quickly than her corpulent body normally allowed. That her veins were coursing with the fire of panic was clear. "Child! We must run! Your grandfather, your father, dead! The Philistines killed them, and David is king!" she cried.

And so it was that the name David was linked to the most horrific event of my life—an event that combined several woes: the deaths of my father, Jonathan, and my grandfather Saul; the end of my life as an honored prince and potential heir to the throne of Israel; and perhaps worst of all, the beginning of my life as a paraplegic.

She hoisted my chubby little body up to rest upon her still-chubbier hip, where I could smell the rank odor of fear-induced sweat pouring from her skin. The door of our quarters was flung open to reveal hordes of my relatives charging down the halls like a herd of wild horses. We pressed into the crowd and ran for the wide door leading out to the palace yard, our own footsteps lost in the clatter of hundreds of sandals upon marble, our screams lost in the wailing that ascended to the high ceilings. The mayhem suspends itself in my mind as I recall the next few moments—my nanny's body lurching forward as she lost her balance, the room spinning as we tumbled to the floor, the wincing pain of my body pinned under hers, and my feet, my tiny feet, *still* tiny feet . . . crushed like two locusts caught under a chariot wheel, so crushed that my sandals were soaked with blood, and yet I flailed at any who tried to help, as if I were warding off a viper attack.

## LO-DEBAR

Lo-debar. To speak the name of my city plunges the voice to its bottom note. *Lo-debar.* Just an obscure town in Gilead south of the sea and north of Jerusalem. Suspended between hope and fear, Lo-debar, just as I was for so many years. I couldn't tear myself away from Judea, for all I ever knew was there, but to live within smelling distance of Jerusalem meant certain execution, so I settled for the place that settled for me, Lo-debar—I don't know what it means.

On the surface you might have called my life normal. I built a house, married, kept up a semblance of survival, sired a son. I learned a trade, bought and sold, slept and ate, talked and listened. But beneath the unremarkable surface, my internal terrain was as jagged and rough as the Aramean mountain peaks where we once traveled during a famine. Not one contented thought ever found a foothold within my heart those long decades, no, never. I hated my life.

Who wouldn't? Not only was I a fugitive, living and hiding and poor, and the offspring of a condemned former king and therefore condemned myself, but I was crippled—there is no pretty way to say it. Eyes filled up with clouds of judgment when they fell upon me as I dragged myself from task to weary task . . . eyes reflecting the judgment of God they knew rested upon me. I could see the muscles around their brows twitch as they tried to surmise what sin put me in such straits. The sad fact was that I took their unspoken word for it—I was an outcast, and I knew it.

Then the messenger that came thundering down the road from Jerusalem one day reminded me that there was one force stronger than my depression, and that was my fear. I hated my life, but I feared my death. I was caught between the torture of living and the fear of dying, like a fly tangled in a spider's web.

"King David has requested your presence at the royal palace. I am to escort you there," the messenger proclaimed. *Funny how he seems almost cheerful carting me off to my doom,* I thought as I bumped along the miles to Jerusalem. Finally the palace appeared, pristine and gleaming in the Judean sun, surrounded by lush gardens. Servants scampered here and there, royal wives strolled in their gorgeous robes, their children playing in flocks as if they were all celebrating a joyful occasion. It all seemed to mock me as I was carried to the throne room. "At least they could have hired one mourner," I whispered under my breath.

As the last corner was rounded, the throne of David came into view. *David.* That name linked with so much that was broken and bleeding in my life—my broken spirit, my broken health, my broken connection to society, my broken feet that never remembered how to grow, that remained ever after twisted and small at the ends of my weak legs. *David.* I heard that name when I recalled with sobs the beaming face of my father, my father whom I still missed even though a father myself. The father whose hand I would gladly have held even now had it been extended to me one more time. No, David had not killed my father, but *David* was the one who took the throne that would have belonged to him. *David.* Now I was approaching the throne of *David,* who still hated me, who wanted me dead, who had already dealt me a living death and now wanted more death. *David.* I saw the luxuriant robe and jewels becoming brighter with each step.

*O God,* I suddenly hoped, *surely there is a bone of mercy some-*

*where in the body of your appointed king. Maybe if I make myself a slave he will spare me . . .*

"Mephibosheth!" his voice resonated as my face met the cold floor at his feet.

"I am your slave!" I retched, with no pride left in me.

The silence that followed was so long that I finally raised my eyes to meet his. There, in eyes I was sure I would find stern justice, I saw something I hadn't seen since looking into the face of my father—in fact, it seemed that David had borrowed the look from my father's memory. Compassion. I saw compassion standing on the rims in the form of tears. "Do not fear," came his voice, "for I am going to treat you with kindness. You see, your father was my best friend, and for his sake I will not only spare you, but I will restore all the land that once belonged to your grandfather Saul."

By now my mouth was open in awe, my eyes blinking foolishly as the royal court stood by watching me. "You will be a great landowner," David continued, "and you will eat at my table on a regular basis." He smiled peacefully.

"Who . . . who am I, your slave, that you should care for a dead dog like me?" I choked. I had never been worth a thing, and now I was being rewarded with riches and honor? What did I do to deserve such blessing?

"Ziba, come." David ignored my question, calling forth a gray old man. "All that belonged to the house of Saul I have given to Mephibosheth." He instructed him to cultivate the land for me and to escort me to the royal table every day. I was to be treated as a prince.

And so it was done, just like that. The command of a king swept away a curse that had hung over me since infancy. Ziba gathered his staff of 20 and his 15 sons, and they set out for Saul's estate in Gibeah, about four miles north of the royal city. In one moment's time I had gone from a condemned criminal to a wealthy prince, and sitting at the royal table with David at the head, I felt like a whole person for the first time since before the accident. My feet were hidden by the table! No one could see them, or judge me because of them.

And so it is with you. You are part of a condemned family, the family of Adam. You have added to your condemnation by committing your own personal sins. You deserve to die, and you know it as you face the King, but there are tears of compassion in His eyes as He tells you that you are part of the royal family, not because you have earned it, but because of the King's love for you. Because of His generosity, you sit at the gospel banqueting table, whole and healthy, restored to favor, as if you had never sinned.

But there is more to the story. We can't accept this gift without being changed by it. Even I was changed—me, the self-absorbed, self-pitying cripple, miraculously turned inside out by the love shown me. And it took a test to make plain this change—that test being the rebellion of Absalom.

It was largely David's fault that the people lost confidence in him. He had become introverted and aloof after his fall with Bathsheba. Oh, he believed he was forgiven, but his former machismo was ground to powder under the boot of moral failure. So he withdrew, and Absalom came to the forefront, stealing the hearts that would have been David's, until finally the climate for revolt was perfect.

And revolt came. While David was in exile, he met with Ziba, my former servant. David asked about me, and the liar told him that I had stayed in Jerusalem, hoping to reap some political rewards if I joined with the rebellion. When David heard this, he resolved to give Ziba my estate when he returned to Jerusalem. Ziba bowed in reverence, I'm sure chuckling under his breath in satisfaction that he had bamboozled the king. The fact that David believed him still has a certain bite to it for me.

After Absalom died at the hand of Joab, and David was reentering Jerusalem, I met him at the river. When David saw me stumbling along, his face registered shock. Was I the defector Ziba claimed I was? David looked at me with jaundiced eye—that is, until he noticed that my mustache was overgrown and my clothes filthy, as if I had been mourning roughly the amount of time he had been in exile. I could sense him wondering if maybe I had been faithful after all.

"Why . . . didn't you go with me, Mephibosheth?" he asked tenuously.

"Why didn't I go with you?" I blurted, trying not to lose all composure. "My Lord, Ziba deceived me! I wanted to saddle a donkey so that I could ride away with you . . . but I'm crippled, re-member?" Catching myself before I lost all sense of reverence, I said, "But you, O king, are like an angel of God. Do whatever is right. I deserved to die, but you treated me like your own son. I have no right to complain."

I could see the king struggling in his mind. Since I was not aware that he had given away my estate to Ziba, I couldn't have understood the question that tensed his brow. But with his next comment, he gave me the clues I needed to piece things together.

"The land will have to be divided, then, between you and Ziba. Can we settle on that?"

*So that's it,* I thought. *David is worried about who will own all the land, the gorgeous, edenic land, which had been mine from the time I loved him. Well, I don't care about the land, because the giver of the land, the source of blessing, is my friend. And my friend is returning to his throne where he belongs. No, I don't care about the land.*

"Let him take it all," I said. "I have you. You have returned to your rightful throne in Jerusalem, and that's what matters to me."

And so David knew that the love he had shown me was re-flected back to him. A smile suddenly broke upon his face, scat-tering the frown, warming my heart. Oh, how sweet came the relief of knowing that David trusted me again.

And likewise, when you receive the love of the King, you will reflect that same love back to Him. And you will never be the same, ever. Your great concern will be seeing Him return from His exile, and your richest reward will be knowing that He trusts you.

Now back to the question of my name—Mephibosheth, "he who scatters shame." I would like to think that my days of doling out shame are over. With all my heart I want to believe that I scat-ter shame in the sense that I send it away like the sunlight scat-ters a pack of rats. How could I do any less, when my Lord has reversed my death sentence, welcomed me to His table, hidden my most embarrassing secret, and given me back everything I lost? Yes, I scatter shame. I hope I have scattered some of yours.

*(Get the story of Mephibosheth for yourself in 2 Samuel 9:1-13; 16:1-4; 19:24-30; and* Patriarchs and Prophets, *page 713.)*

## COGITATIONS

1. What core belief did Mephibosheth have concerning David while he was in Lo-debar? How did this core belief affect him?

2. Have you had similar core beliefs concerning God? How have they affected you?

3. First Corinthians 7:23 says, "You were bought with a price; do not become slaves of men" (NASB). Sometimes we become "slaves" to what people think of us. How does this affect our sense of self-worth? How can the fact that we were "bought with a price" free us?

# Stella Goes for the Gold

*"Do you not know that those who run in a race all run, but only one receives the prize? Run in such a way that you may win."*

1 CORINTHIANS 9:24, NASB.

The Olympics began in 776 B.C. in Olympia, Greece, a valley lush with olive trees. There was just one race—a 192-meter dash, which was won by a cook. Today the Olympics are a 3,000-hour-long media marathon, which more than 60 percent of the world watches on the tube.

# I Want It All

Competing in the Olympics is an increasingly rule-bound experience. The first Olympics had few rules (one of which was that the contestants had to parade naked at the outset of the race—no thanks!), but today the rules have multiplied along with the gold medalist wannabes. Many have been the cheaters who have broken the steroid bans on the sly, but there is one fake that takes the cake.

Polish contestant Stella Walsh competed in the 1932 Los Angeles Olympics and won the 100-meter dash. Stella rode on the waves of glory and fame until 48 years later when an autopsy revealed that Stella Walsh was a *man.**

So passionately did she—er, *he*—want that gold medal that he, whatever his real name was, was willing to sell out his gender identity in order to get it.

We are willing to do so much in order to distinguish ourselves, but so often our way of winning ends in compromise. Far better is God's plan of giving us a sense of worth. When we win with Him, we don't make anyone a loser, not even ourselves.

## TRY IT OUT

1. Next time your church has a vesper program, volunteer to make a 10-minute presentation. Dress in a robe and sandals and, after walking out with a limp, read the story of Mephibosheth.

2. Read "God's Love for Man" from the book *Steps to Christ.*

3. Set aside $2 as offering money and put each dollar in a paperback copy of *Steps to Christ* or other small witnessing book. Make sure the dollar bill sticks out. The next time you pass a toll booth, give them to the person in the booth and say, "Take one for yourself and give one to the person in the car behind me."

4. Think of someone who feels like an outcast, and spend a moment putting yourself in their shoes. Buy them a small gift or help them in some way every day and watch as their attitude brightens.

## CROSS-EXAMINE THE WITNESS

*Our witness is Rachel Matthews from the Black Hills area in South Dakota, where she home-schools. Rachel is a great storyteller.*

QUESTION: WHAT IS YOUR SOURCE OF SELF-WORTH?

I was a slave to fears of what strangers thought of me. I didn't feel the need to change in order to impress my friends, because I knew that they accepted me as I was, but I feared what the people on the street or in the stores thought. The people that seemed to "have it all" when it came to fashion and music were the ones I found intimidating.

Looking back, I realize that I didn't dress oddly, but I felt out of place—as if people stared at me because I dressed *slightly* different. A phobia grew in my mind that people thought I looked weird. I knew nothing of the popular brands of clothing, and because of financial limitations I was not able to wear designer clothes. My fears, among other things, drove me into a deep depression.

Finally the light dawned. I began to understand that the people on the street didn't care about me. They probably didn't notice me, and I would probably never see them again. I began to come out of my depression and realize that my true self-worth is not found in whether or not I knew the latest songs from the Backstreet Boys, or whether my closet is full of expensive clothes. My only source of true self-worth comes from my Father in heaven. He loves me for exactly who I am.

---

\* Ken McAlpinen, "Faster, Higher, Stronger," *American Way,* July 15, 1996, pp. 59, 60.

# Mrs. Thunder

*"But you, are you seeking great things for yourself? Do not seek them."*

JEREMIAH 45:5, NASB.

*other hen . . . stage mother . . . smother mother . . .* oh, go ahead—add *Jewish* mother to the list. What can I say? They were my sons, and I wanted them to prosper.

Oh, and the name. No, I was not really "Mrs. Thunder." I was the wife of Zebedee, and my sons were the *sons* of Zebedee until Jesus gave them the nickname "Sons of Thunder." Then I became, to those who liked to chide me, "Mrs. Thunder." Why the thunder? Probably referring to the temperament of the family. Let's just say we were not known for our quiet dinner table conversation. We talked loudly, emoted freely, and argued our fair share. All in all, it was done with affection and deep devotion to one another, but a more gentle bystander might not have understood that.

It was a bit of a blow to hear that the boys were giving up the fishing business to follow Jesus of Nazareth. We had worked so hard to build our name. Finally we were prospering to the point of having our own servants and entering into a partnership with Simon. Things were good. I was able to buy the fine silks from India I had always longed for, wearing them on special occasions and enjoying the compliments. Like any mother, I had hopes of my sons marrying good Jewish girls and bringing me grandchildren to pleasure me in my old age. I wanted the boys to be at least as successful as their father, and preferably bypass him in earning power and standing in society. We were part of a very divided culture, in which the rich were the only ones allowed privileges, and the poor were thought to exist only to serve and bless the rich. So the only way you could have a life was to get out of poverty and into wealth. Living, for us, was a scramble to get to a higher plane of existence. Can you blame us for trying? Yet it was not to be. My successful sons left their business to follow a Teacher who lived like a wilderness prophet.

This is how it all happened. Jesus was walking by the Sea of Galilee (or the Lake of Gennesaret, as they call it) with a multitude of ogle-eyed followers. He spotted Simon and the boys washing their nets. Jesus asked Simon, our business partner, if He could use his boat, which He ended up using as a preaching platform for the crowd. When the speech was over, Jesus told Simon to come out to the boat and let down his nets again. You've already heard the story, I'm sure. The nets were full to the point of breaking.

This was clearly a miracle. They never caught any fish in those waters that time of day. Simon realized that he was in the presence of God, and fell on his knees. Then the recruitment appeal came. Jesus would give them all a promotion to the position of "fishers of men," as He called it. How could they refuse? I'm sure you're tempted to think that they had shekel signs in their eyes and hopes of worldly honor, but I think not. I think they sensed even then that it would cost them all to follow this teacher from Nazareth. And still they followed.

Oh, so many more miracles came. The stilling of the storm waters of the lake. Healings—including the daughter of Jairus, a synagogue ruler. The boys' first evangelistic crusade. Simon walking on water. The Transfiguration; the raising of Lazarus. And of course the vicious persecution of the Jewish authorities—friends of mine, some of them! There was never a moment of boredom, but the stress was worth it. The more time we spent with Jesus, the more we loved Him, and the more convinced we were that He was the Son of God.

Then He dropped the bomb. After three years of ministry,

when the Passover was drawing near, He told His 12 that this visit to Jerusalem would bring His arrest. He would be delivered to the Gentiles, mocked, spit upon, scourged, and put to death. Then, He said, He would rise on the third day. It didn't really register as reality. The man was only 33 years old, and here he was facing death! And the boys had just finished telling thousands, "The kingdom of heaven is at hand" (Matthew 10:7, NASB). He had promised that we would sit with Abraham, Isaac, and Jacob, that we would have a hundredfold of the houses and lands that we had forsaken for Him! It was all too confusing.

The hardest part was the thought of losing Jesus. John, my dear John, loving boy that He was, was right next to Him every chance he got. James watched for His blessing as a lamb bleats for a handful of grain. Their hearts were just as pierced as mine were with all this talk of Him dying! All we could think of was how we wanted to be connected to Him, to be honored of Him, to be identified with Him.

We decided upon a plan. We knew His kingdom would come eventually, so the boys and I would go to Jesus and request the thrones on His right and on His left. If this request was granted, there might be a conflict over who got which side, the right side being the more honorable position, but we would deal with that later. First we must make sure that our good family got the proper recognition in this new kingdom.

"Teacher, we have a favor to ask," we said.

"What can I do for you?" Jesus was His usual polite self.

"Let us each have a place, one on Your right side and one on Your left, in Your future kingdom!" the boys pleaded, their passionate feelings driving the volume of their voices.

"You don't know what you are asking for," came Jesus' reply. "Are you able to be baptized with My baptism?"

The boys weren't positive what that meant, but they assumed that it meant that they would be called to suffer.

The other disciples, who had overheard the whole conversation, were furious. I can see now why they were, knowing that we were trying to aggrandize ourselves that way. The conflict didn't escalate as it could have, however, because Jesus spoke to all 12. He let them know the conditions of position in His kingdom:

"The Gentile rulers lord it over the poor and powerless. This is not the way I want you to operate. If you want to be great, then become a servant. If you want to be first, become a slave. Even I, the Son of man, came to serve others, to the point of laying down My life to save the world."

There was a thoughtful silence after these words were spoken. I think we all began to conceive of the difference between the laws of the world's kingdom and the laws of God's. While the world was full of people trying to pull themselves up higher, God's kingdom was full of servants. Giving, not getting, was the highest privilege. You couldn't politic your way into position in God's kingdom, because it was based upon how self-giving you were.

Let me tell you how things ended up. Jesus was indeed crucified. I watched the whole ordeal along with Mary Magdalene and others. It was when Jesus' mother came to be with Him in His dying moment that I had a chance to apply the lesson of self-sacrifice that Jesus had spoken of. With labored breath He asked Mary to adopt John and John to adopt Mary. And so my son acquired another mother. I could have regarded the whole thing as a put-down, as if I had been replaced or something, but as I looked upon the dying form of the Son of God I thought, *No, no. Let go of your Son. Let this poor, forlorn woman enjoy him.* God gave His *only* Son—couldn't I give *one* of mine?

Actually, I gave the other as well. The persecution that began with Jesus continued with His church. We lived like animals, darting from haven to haven, attempting to escape the ire of the Jewish leaders and Herod. Out of a desire to appease the Jews, Herod had my son James put to death with the sword.

So what do I have to say in retrospect? That I have found the way to achieve that significance, that status, that we all naturally want. It's easy—you simply cease to want it. Yes, you heard me right—you cease to want it! You see, I as a Jewish mother had looked to my sons to give me a sense of feeling important. In the midst of my pursuit of importance, however, I learned something *more* important. I learned the law of God's kingdom. You live for others, not yourself. You are driven by true love, not the false love that steps on people to get higher. Once I had grasped this, I was willing to give up, to let go of, that which was all-consuming to me—namely, my sons. The wonder of all this is that when I stopped trying to make them successful, they became supremely successful. One became an adoptive son of the Lord's mother, and the other one of the first Christian martyrs.

Who knows what John will go on to become in his remaining days? There is talk of him writing out the story of Jesus. Maybe he will become a great author, who can say? I may not be around to see it happen, but I will meet him in the kingdom and find out. Oh, and I don't care if he has a throne on the right or left side of Jesus. I only want to hear that he gave all for the One who gave all for him. That is enough to make this mother very, very proud.

*(Get the story of Mrs. Thunder yourself in Matthew 4:20-22; Mark 1:20; Luke 5:10; Matthew 26:27-36; Mark 3:14-19; 10:35-45; Matthew 20:20-28; 27:55, 56; Acts 12:1, 2; and* The Desire of Ages, *pages 547-551.)*

## COGITATIONS

1. Is it normal for mothers to want their children to succeed? When does this become a bad thing?

2. There are two basic types of love: human love and divine love. Human love is self-centered, but divine love is self-giving. The Zebedees had divine love for Jesus (see *The Desire of Ages*, p. 548), but it was tainted with their humanity. In view of this, how did Jesus respond to their desire to be on His right and left hand?

3. In what constructive way can you deal with Christians who are seeking honor and glory for self? How can you deal with *yourself* when you do the same thing?

# Star Suicides

The 1990s brought forth a strange phenomenon—an unprecedented rate of suicide among rock-and-roll stars. Probably the only name that pops into your mind is Kurt Cobain, the singer/songwriter/frontman of the rock band Nirvana, who took his life at the height of his band's popularity in 1994. All the other suicides were stars who had passed into obscurity—in fact, the loss of popularity was the reason for the suicide in most cases:

Michael Hutchence, the lead singer of the Australian band INXS, immensely popular in the 1980s, found his vanished fame to be too much to take.

Doug Hopkins, guitarist/songwriter for the Gin Blossoms, committed suicide after being fired from the band, presumably for drug abuse.

Chris Acland, drummer for the British band Lush, killed himself after their 1996 tour, probably because of a failed romance.

Rob Pilatus, the former star of Milli Vanilli, the duo who were found to be only good-looking lip-syncers (they didn't sing their own songs), met with an "accidental" drug overdose, which could have been intentional, since he had attempted to overdose only a few months before.[1]

And the list goes on . . .

It's not hard to conceive of someone who has tasted the euphoria of fame, and has been worshiped by thousands, losing their purpose in life once that fame is gone. But Kurt Cobain had it all—fame, fortune, and the respect of the "Nirvana generation." Why did he *end* it all when he *had* it all?

Because he realized, once he had it "all," that "all" wasn't so great after all. "All" was empty. "All" was lonely. "All" was a life of wealth, pleasure, and pride, and if Kurt Cobain did nothing else, he proved that people are not made truly happy by these things. We seek the good things of life in order to distinguish ourselves, to feel significant, but true significance comes when we serve others, not when we ourselves are served. If Kurt had taken the claims of God upon his soul seriously, and had tried to use his immense popularity and talent to bless others with a knowledge of the gospel, he would be alive today.

Contrast Kurt Cobain with another musician—a Christian named Steve Green. Green has been called a long-distance runner in a world of sprinters, referring to the sometimes faddish Christian music industry, where popularity can come and go as fast as a summer storm. Green has remained active through the ebb and flow of his own popularity, because he is in music ministry not for the recognition, but for the ministry. Not that he hasn't been extremely successful—Steve Green has 18 number one songs, six GMA Dove Awards, and four Grammy nominations to his credit—but service to others is the main focus for this powerful singer.

It hasn't always been so. In Steve's early career he was, in his own words, "a voice for hire. I sang for my own satisfaction or the approval of others, but my heart wasn't right." As his fame increased, Steve's spiritual condition worsened. "The gap between the image I portrayed and the true condition of my heart was widening. I was dangerously deceived." Then came a painful confrontation from Steve's older brother, which led to the singer's conversion. A total change in his approach to ministry came about. "At the concerts now, people were souls, perhaps some with great need. I would stare at the audience, concerned that they truly understood the gospel. That was the beginning of ministry for me."[2]

All of us want to have some kind of significance, but it's deceptive to think that this comes through fame, fortune, or other attainments. True significance comes in serving others, in meeting a real need using the talents we have. If only Kurt Cobain had known.

*"He who has found his life will lose it, and he who has lost his life for My sake will find it."*

MATTHEW 10:39, NASB.

## TRY IT OUT

1. Take a one-hour walk with the express purpose of thinking about what your ministry is in life. Ask such questions as: What are my talents? What do I love to do? What will make the most difference?

2. Pose these questions to several friends, and perhaps an adult or two: What do you feel my talents are? What kind of ministry could I be successful in?

3. Volunteer for a day at a local soup kitchen, clothing distribution program, or other charitable organization. See how it makes you feel.

## CROSS-EXAMINE THE WITNESS

 *Our witness is Leilana Joy Boykin, a home-schooler from McEwen, Tennessee. Leilana enjoys playing both guitar and piano.*

QUESTION: WHERE DO YOU FIND TRUE SIGNIFICANCE?

I find true significance in helping others come to know Jesus better. Selling truth-filled books and passing out literature helps me know that I am doing something that will make a difference.

Nearly all mothers want their children to succeed. It's just a natural thing. My mom wants me to succeed, because she loves me and wants the best for me. Sometimes, though, this can become a bad thing. For instance, some mothers want their children to succeed so badly that they flaunt their talents and put them on display, and cause their children to think, *I'm so great!* The children become proud and vain, and they forget God and His love for them and how they can serve others.

## I Want It All

Some people, as we see in the story of the Zebedees, want earthly gain, honor, and glory for themselves. We need to show them by our own lives that the true and happy way is found not in making a show, but in doing what we can to benefit others and bring happiness to them. God will then honor us in ways that we don't even expect. When I begin wanting significance in this world, I must ask Him to help me not to focus on myself but to look away from myself to Jesus, and then ask Him whom I can bless. This brings true significance.

---

[1] "The List of Nine," Aug. 10, 1998, www.forcor.com/list9-0811.html.

[2] Steve Green Ministries Web site, "Biography," www.stevegreenministries.org/Biography.html.

# The Apothecary Owner

*"He poured out Himself to death, and was numbered with the transgressors."*

ISAIAH 53:12, NASB.

My lifelong goal could be summed up in a word: money. My father was a successful businessman, my grandfather was a successful businessman, my uncles were successful businessmen, and it was understood that *I* would be a successful business-man. I worked in the apothecary until my father passed away, when I inherited it along with most of his bank account and the stock of the store. Some of the perfumes we carried were so expensive that I kept them buried in a chest in my home above the shop. When you consider the cost of the stock plus my savings, I was loaded. This all made me very happy, until one day I met a woman who led me to question my priorities.

Judging by the looks of her, she was the wife of a poor farmer. Not a lavishly dressed woman, probably coming in to buy a cheap bottle of perfume as a small gift. The bread and butter of the business comes from the accumulation of these small sales, so I treated her with respect even though I didn't want the sale to take very long.

"Sir, I would like a bottle of perfume," she began, as if I didn't know that. Actually, I was taken aback for a moment as I focused on her face. She was a lovely woman, someone whom I would ex-pect to be married to a wealthier man, but then her clothes were so plain that I knew it couldn't be.

"I want it to be very . . . special," she said, as if giving me some highly secret piece of information. *No, woman, you want your gift to be nonspecial, so you can say to the receiver, "Here, I just wanted you to know how nonspecial you are!"*

"Of course you want it to be special!" I said, smiling my most jubilant smile. "Everything I have is special!" I made a sweeping motion around my store.

Her eyes darted around the room a bit, as if she was watching for spies. "I mean special as in expensive," she said.

*OK, OK, you have a few shekels burning a hole in your pocket and you think you are going to bump me into early retirement; is that it?*

"I certainly have many expensive perfumes in this store!" I said. "What is your price range, madam?" I spoke charmingly, if I do say so myself.

"I would like to see your most expensive perfume," she said, poker-faced.

I could hardly stifle my laughter. *Right, right! My most expensive perfume would put you in such debt that you would be forced to prostitute yourself in order to pay it back!*

"Madam, my most expensive perfume is probably out of your price range," I said, "but . . . let me show you something . . ." I took a bottle off the shelf. It was a simple-scented olive oil in a blue-glazed clay flask, which cost just a little more than a loaf of bread. I smiled benevolently as I held it out to her, but she just looked at it with her brows furrowed.

"How much?"

"Madam, it costs only two brass shekels," I said.

"No, no," she shook her head. I put the flask back and was about to reach for something on the lowest shelf, when she reached out and put her hands on my shoulders as if to steady me. Peering into my eyes she said, "I want something *really* expensive."

I looked at her for quite some time. As beautiful as she was, there was a hardness in her face, an exhaustion, as if woe had left a trail of lines. Her eyes held a deep intensity, an intelligence I had never before seen in a farmer's wife. I began to feel that there was some saga behind this woman, a drama belied by her simple attire.

Cautiously I revealed the more expensive items in my store to her, one by one. The simple but elegant oleander rose oil from the flower that grows around the ruins of Jericho, which I picked myself and extracted in a bag press. The sandalwood and the lotus ointments from India in their jeweled cases. The frankincense and spice concoction in an ebony box, imported from Arabia. The price of the treasures climbed higher, higher, as she refused them one by one. Finally I leveled with her.

"Madam, are you playing some kind of game with me? I do not often have, uh, common customers demand my most expensive products. Usually an appointment must be made to see the top of the line. It is, you know, a bit of a security issue to have the most valuable items brought out during business hours. The streets of Jerusalem are filled with thugs . . ." I paused, hoping she would be honest with me about her intentions.

The woman looked at me again with those thoughtful eyes. They were just too serious to be searching for folly. "I'm sorry I didn't make an appointment," she said. "Can I make one now?"

I walked to the door of my shop, taking a long look down the street both ways. Not seeing anything of importance, I hung out the "closed" sign and locked my shop door. Coming back to the mystery woman, I handed her a tablet, asking her to write her name and address. Satisfied that she was authentic, I excused myself and walked into the storeroom behind the shop. I came back with a large silver urn overlaid with mother-of-pearl in a design resembling grapevines. It was carefully wrapped in purple silk, which I laid out on the table, placing the urn in its midst.

"This is fine myrrh from the Orient, rare and sweet, madam," I said, dipping the tip of my finger into the urn and passing it under her nose.

She closed her eyes as if to recall something, smiled slightly, and asked, as always, "How much?"

"Madam, I am a bit embarrassed to say—"

"Say on."

## I Want It All

"Madam, the cost is 100 denarii, more than you are prepared to pay, I'm sure . . . However, if you—"

"Sir," she interrupted, "I can pay *more* than that. Do you have anything *more* valuable?"

This time I did laugh. I could hardly believe that this plainly clad woman could afford *more* than most statesmen and princes. "Madam, I hope you aren't insulted by this question, but . . . what is your occupation, that you have such means?"

At this her eyes fell quickly to the floor. After a long pause she looked at me again and said, "I am a disciple of a great teacher, Jesus of Nazareth, whom I believe is the Messiah. I was once a harlot, a *successful* harlot. I saved enough money to buy myself whatever I wanted, but found after I met Him that I wanted nothing *but* Him. I know from my Jewish upbringing that the money earned in harlotry is not to be used as an offering to God. The Law of Moses does not say, however, that something *bought* with that money can't be given. Jesus has said that He will die soon at the hand of the Romans. I want to provide the burial ointment. Sir, have you ever loved someone so much that you were willing to give everything you have?"

I'm sure I blushed deeply at this question, but only after the moment it took even to comprehend it. *Why, no,* I thought, *I have never given much of anything. I love to see the accumulation of riches too much to give many of them away.*

"Madam, I am prepared to show you the finest item that I have. You must promise, however, not to disclose to any soul that I even own such a priceless treasure. Do I have your word?" I asked.

"You have my word."

I climbed the ladder into my house above the shop, walked into the last room and dug through the cedar chest until I laid my hands on my single most valuable possession, a white alabaster box wrapped in red velvet. Within a few minutes I was with her again, laying the red velvet cloth on my counter. I carefully placed the glistening white box before her.

Madam," I began, then thought better. Looking for the tablet,

I read her name. *"Mary!"*

Yes!" Se smiled at the sound of her name.

This is an alabaster box filled with spikenard, a perfume oil from the *Nardostachys jatamansi* flower, which can be found only in the Himalayas. This exquisite ointment has a fragrance so powerful that it will seem to fill the universe when the box is broken. But I can't allow you to sample it, madam . . . *Mary,* because once this box is broken, it can never be resealed. It is meant to be given as an extravagant demonstration of adoration and homage to a great king."

The moment the word "king" escaped my lips, she spoke, "How much?"

"Three hundred denarii," I said.

Upon hearing this, she fetched a small cloth bag from the folds of her robe. Untying the drawstring, she opened the mouth of the bag and poured out more gold coins than I had seen in months—a full year's wages at least. After counting the coins carefully, earnestly, she stood back like a proud little soldier.

"Three hundred, exactly, and not a shekel to spare. Give me the box, sir, and I thank you for your time."

Not a shekel to spare. The woman had spent her life savings. If a queen had bought it, it would have barely dented her storehouse, but this woman was left with nothing. I had never seen anything like it! In a world in which every soul was engaged in a constant effort to make themselves richer, she had made herself poor so that she could make this Jesus of Nazareth rich. My skin tingled with the mystery of it all. I carefully folded the box in the red velvet cloth, then wrapped the bundle in a piece of plain linen, placing it in her upturned hands. She held the parcel as a child holds a long-chased butterfly, utterly pleased with herself and her purchase. I walked to the door of the shop and unlocked it, watching her pass before me, still wondering what possessed her. Then, summoning my courage, I asked, "Madam, uh, *Mary,* how might I meet this Jesus of Nazareth?"

*(Get the story of the apothecary owner and Mary Magdalene for yourself in Matthew 26:6-9; Mark 14:3-5; Luke 7:37, 38; John 12:1-5; and* The Desire of Ages, *pages 559-568.)*

## COGITATIONS

1. This is a mostly fictional account of what might have happened when Mary bought the ointment. How do you envision the event?

2. Why do you think the disciples, especially Judas, reacted so negatively to Mary's generosity?

3. The essence of Mary's gift was that it was so generous it appeared impractical. Allow yourself the blessing of doing something impractical and generous. Give money away, clean an elderly person's house for nothing, pick all the losing players for your basketball team. Whatever you can do to bless someone else in an "unreasonable" way, do it.

# Get-(Un)Rich-Quick Schemes

*"Give, and it will be given to you; good measure, pressed down, shaken together running over they will pour into your lap. For whatever measure you deal out to others, it will be dealt to you in return."*

LUKE 6:38, NASB.

ne of the most prestigious positions a person can hold is to be on *Forbes* magazine's list of the top 25 richest Americans. Someone such as Bill Gates, worth between $50 and $100 billion, has no trouble staying high on that list—in fact, he was the richest man in the world in the year 2000. If John D. Rockefeller could rise from the dead and hop in a time tunnel, though, Bill Gates would have to eat sour grapes and step down to second place. In 1913 Rockefeller's fortune was $900 million, equivalent to nearly $200 billion in today's money. Now, that's what you call a billionaire.[1]

But there is something truly amazing in the Rockefeller story. By 1922 he had given away $1 billion to his family and to charity, keeping just $20 million to himself. (I know, *only* $20 million! It must have been hard . . . )[2] Following in his footsteps, Ted Turner announced in 1997 that he would donate $1 billion of his $3.2 billion estate to the United Nations for "refugees, cleaning up land mines, peacekeeping, UNICEF for the children, . . . diseases."[3] Likewise, philanthropist Doris Bryant, known as the "Sunshine Lady," has awarded $3 million from her foundation to various causes, to "spread a kindly light on the world." The greatest philanthropist of all time is Andrew Carnegie, who distributed most of his fortune to public-library construction and the setting up of other educational institutions. Today he would be worth more than $50 billion. That's a lot of books.[4]

**133**

# I Want It All

These givers realized something of Jesus' teaching on wealth. In a nutshell, Jesus told us that a person's wealth is determined, not by what they hold on to, but by what they give away. "Give, and it will be given unto you," He said, not meaning that our charity would make us richer, but that for all we gave away, we would receive something much more precious. What could be more precious than a few mil (or bil)? A chance to feel His Spirit move upon you. A taste of what Jesus experienced when He gave all He had. The awareness that someone was helped by something you did. How can you put a price tag on these things?

The greatest gift of all is the experience of giving. Give while you have anything to give, and God will make sure that you don't regret it.

---

[1] *Guinness Book of World Records 2000* (Stamford, Conn.: Guinness World Records Ltd., 2000), p. 70.

[2] *Ibid.*

[3] "Ted Turner Donates $1 Billion to 'UN Causes,'" www.cnn.com/us/9709/18/turner.gift.

[4] *Guinness Book of World Records 2000,* p. 68.

# The Dream

*"I count all things to be loss in view of the surpassing value of know-ing Christ Jesus my Lord, for whom I have suffered the loss of all things, and count them but rubbish in order that I may gain Christ . . . that I may know Him, and the power of His resurrection and the fellowship of His sufferings, being conformed to His death."*

PHILIPPIANS 3:8-10, NASB.

ast night I dreamed that I was taken on angel wing to the gates of heaven. We spun through the atmosphere, through silky clouds and swirling stars, until at last the angel set me down, saying, "This is your destination—an eternity of peace."

I have never been surrounded with such beauty before. The air was filled with rich music. The sky was a bluest blue. The path that led to the gate was studded with jewels and hedged with flowers. The gate itself was of such exquisite structure and material that I couldn't take my eyes off it until the angel spoke. Then my eyes fell upon the most beautiful thing of all— a being of such physical power and loveliness that the sight of it made me gasp.

"This is your home," the angel spoke, holding out a hand to-ward the open gate. A soft yet glorious light poured through that gate, reflecting off everything and filling the angel's eyes. I felt al-most irresistibly drawn in to the place of light, to the source of the lush music, and I had nearly walked through the open gate when the angel spoke again.

"You are welcome to enter. You must know, however, that Jesus is not there."

*What? Heaven without Jesus? How could this be?* I thought

"Jesus is still on the cross—hanging over there between two

thieves on the hill Golgotha," the angel said sadly, pointing in the opposite direction. As my gaze followed his pointing finger, I saw a hill in the distance surrounded by weeping clouds. Three crosses stood like dead, leafless trees. On the middle was my Jesus, my dear Jesus, crying out to God in agony, not able to sense the favor of God or see the light behind the glorious gate.

My eyes turned again to the beauty of the gate and the angel who stood there. Oh, the drawing I felt to this perfectly happy place, but the strange pull I felt to the hill Golgotha where the Master of heaven hung dying.

My mind argued with itself, saying, *You can't help Him by going to Golgotha. He would want you to go and enjoy the good things of eternity until He can join you.*

Then, *No, no! What is heaven without Heaven personified? How could I enjoy the bliss of a perfect place knowing that He is still suffering?*

My eyes flashed back and forth between the ugly cross and the beautiful gate. My ears tuned in and out of cries of pain and angel songs. Where would I go? What would I do? My feet pointed toward Golgotha. I would go to Jesus.

I woke up in a sweat, immediately breathing a sigh of relief. "It was only a dream," I said.

## TRY IT OUT

1. If you ever go on a short-term mission trip, ask God to show you a need in the place where you minister. When you get home, ask your area churches if you can take 15 minutes of mission report time and talk about your trip. Show slides of the trip, then ask that an offering be taken for you to send to the people. Have a goal in mind before you start and tell the church what it is—such as "I'm collecting $500 for art supplies for the orphanage."

2. The next time a worthy ministry presents itself, give away all the money you have to it. I dare you.

# CROSS-EXAMINE THE WITNESS

*Our witness is Miles Merwin, from Connecticut. Miles would like to be a farmer or an aviator, but for now he is content to do such things as backpacking, biking, and playing piano and violin. Miles has traveled many miles to share the love of God with others, as you will see.*

QUESTION: WHAT PART DOES MONEY HAVE IN THE LIVES OF CHRISTIANS WAITING FOR THE COMING OF CHRIST?

Material things affect Christians. Some Christians are rich and others are not so rich, but every Christian can get carried away with the riches of this world. Money is a big issue in the lives of Christians waiting for the coming of Christ. Some Christians think we have money just to buy things for ourselves, but God asks us to share.

I have gone to Honduras twice on short-term mission trips and have enjoyed them a lot. I encourage you to go on a short-term mission trip if you have a chance—you will not regret it. I believe we made some lives happier. The purpose of our trips was to meet medical needs and build churches. We raised money for the medicines and the church building supplies before we went. Both times the pharmacy ran out of money, and both times the volunteers donated their own money to buy more medicines.

The things God blesses us with are not just to be enjoyed, but to be shared.

# The Old Prophet

*"To the law and to the testimony! If they do not speak according to this word, it is because they have no dawn."*

Isaiah 8:20, NASB.

Y ou probably don't know me by any name other than "the old prophet," so that will have to do for now. You will find my story buried in the beginning of 1 Kings, couched in between Solomon and Elijah. The stories of that period tend to be convoluted and tedious, the way things get when we shut God out of our lives. I am writing now as a sort of confessional. My sin is lying, but hearing my story may help you along in your quest for truth.

It all began a short time after Solomon's death. Solomon's son Rehoboam, heir to the throne, was the product of a very dysfunctional home. For starters, Solomon had 700 wives and 300 concubines. That's 1,000 women competing for his affections—he probably didn't spend much time with young Rehoboam. As a result of this lack of fathering, Rehoboam had some serious setbacks. One was that he was an ineffective leader. When an innovator named Jeroboam came along, the people favored him. In the end 10 of the tribes went with Jeroboam, and only two stayed with Solomon's son.

But Jeroboam had his own set of problems, namely idolatry. Jeroboam had built an altar in Bethel with a golden calf, which he claimed had delivered the people from Egypt. A certain prophet from Judah went to warn the king that God's judgment was about to fall. The altar, he said, would be the future execution place of the false priests of Israel. As a sign that this would come to pass, the prophet said, the altar would split and the ashes would pour out.

The king was completely enraged. He drew his hand out of his robe and pointed with a shaking finger at the one who was exposing his sin. "Seize him!" he screeched, but the moment the words split the air his eyes moved from the prophet to his own hand, which was suspended in midair. It had literally dried up like a fish lying on the shore of the Dead Sea, and he was unable to move it.

At that moment, as the shriveled hand hung in the air, the altar split open and the ashes poured out, just as the prophecy said. What greater evidence could God give that this prophet knew what he was talking about? The king had a sudden conversion, and begged the prophet to pray that the hand would be healed, which happened instantly. Once the king regained his composure and brushed a few ash flakes off his robe with his restored hand, he cleared his throat and gave the prophet a dinner invitation. A very awkward situation was behind them, and he was determined to try to brighten things up socially.

When the prophet gave him a firm no, the king was stunned, unaccustomed to being turned down for such things, but the prophet explained that it was by direct command of God that he not eat or drink until he returned from his mission. Jeroboam had a newfound respect for God, so he didn't argue much.

When my sons, who saw the whole altar/dried-hand fiasco, returned with the story of what had happened, I was intrigued with this austere prophet who carried out his mission with such exactitude. *He did nice work,* I thought. *He's probably worth getting to know. Besides, we prophets need to stick together. There are certain things in the life of a prophet that no one but a prophet can understand.*

Mulling over all this, I decided on a plan. "Which way did he go?" I asked my sons, then told them to saddle a donkey for me.

# I Want It All

Within minutes I was off to meet a new friend. I found him sitting under an oak tree. "Are you the man of God who came from Judah?" I asked

"I am," he said.

"Come home with me and eat!" I said enthusiastically.

I cannot return with you," he said solemnly, explaining that God had commanded him to return home without stopping to eat. Whew, this fellow took his job seriously. As I pondered the matter, I concluded that what he really needed was to loosen up a bit, to live a little. Getting him to do that, however, was not going to be an easy task. I could see it in the expression on his face—he stared forward with his brow furled slightly, as if trying to ward off distractions. But as focused as this fellow was, I thought I detected something else . . . yes, a certain neediness, a loneliness, a desire for camaraderie.

"I'm a prophet like you," I said gently. His face softened at that moment, and I saw that under the flint he was putty. I continued with a bold-faced lie: "An angel spoke to me by the word of the Lord, saying, 'Bring him back with you to your house, that he may eat bread and drink water'" (1 Kings 13:18, NASB).

I could almost see the man's salivary glands pulse at the mention of food and water. It's hard work rebuking kings, and a guy builds up quite an appetite—how well I know. I felt satisfied that I had him in the palm of my hand now, but there was a tinge of guilt in my soul that I should have paid attention to.

"Well, OK," the prophet said softly.

We had a rather quiet journey home, but as we sat at the table the fellow opened up a little. At first it was chitchat—the weather, politics, the economy—but eventually things got more serious, and the two of us were able to talk shop. Prophet shop.

Suddenly I began to sense that I was about to be used to speak. The word of the Lord came forcefully into my mind, and I said, "Thus says the Lord, 'Because you have disobeyed the command of the Lord, and have . . . eaten . . . and drunk . . . in a place . . . He said . . . [not to], your body shall not come to the grave of your fathers.'" Basically, this meant that my prophet friend was going to die. A sober silence came between us. The man knew he had done wrong in succumbing to me, and what's more, he knew I lied to him. But as much of a disappointment as the whole affair had been so far, it didn't come close to what happened next.

After he had ridden away and was gone for some time, some men came shouting at my door. "The prophet from Judah has been mauled by a lion, and is dead on the side of the road!" My nerves were ratcheted up into high gear. I rode as fast as my donkey could bump along, finally seeing the prophet's donkey and the lion in the distance standing beside a shadow on the road. I couldn't bear to look, but I couldn't turn away. Slowly I rode forward until I saw him there, lying in a pool of blood. The lion didn't budge. He looked almost sorry himself.

With tears of remorse I picked up the dead body and tenderly laid it across the back of my donkey. "Oh, how could I have done this?" I wondered, and still do. I buried the man in my own grave, requesting of my sons that I be laid next to him when the time came. I know that I deserve to be where he is.

Friends and truth-seekers, there are liars out there. I was one of them. And we don't wear signs that say "I fib," either. Liars can even be prophets and others in important positions. How can you shield yourself? Take it from me, a reformed fraud. Compare everything with the Word of God. If my prophet friend had done that, he would be alive today.

*(Get the story of the old prophet for yourself in 1 Kings 13.)*

## COGITATIONS

1. Is it possible to question authority respectfully? Name some historical figures who have done this.

2. Does newly discovered truth disagree with established truth?

3. Is it possible to lie in order to help someone?

# Brainwashed

*"Therefore, prepare your minds for action, keep sober in spirit, fix your hope completely on the grace to be brought to you at the revelation of Jesus Christ."*

1 PETER 1:13, NASB.

an Francisco, California, February 1974. A shower of gunfire tore through a building, and several kidnappers absconded with a beautiful 19-year-old girl. Patricia Hearst was the daughter of the wealthy Randolph Hearst, whose company owned several media outlets such as *Harper's Bazaar* and *Cosmopolitan* magazines. Her kidnappers were the Symbionese Liberation Army, a radical leftist group whose motto was "Death to the fascist insect that preys upon the life of the people."[1] Definitely not a mild-mannered bunch.

The SLA told Patty's father that they would return his daughter if he would give $6 million to feed the poor of California. Although he met this demand, Randolph Hearst still didn't see or hear from his daughter until she sent him a message that read: "I hear that people all around the country keep calling on the SLA to release me unharmed. But the SLA are not the ones who are harming me. It's the FBI along with your indifference to the poor."[2] Three weeks later Hearst heard from his daughter again, and this time she informed him that she had joined the SLA. Two months after the kidnapping, Patty had changed her name to Tania and was seen wielding a carbine (a large gun) during the holdup of a San Francisco bank.

It doesn't take a Ph.D. in psychology to figure out what happened to Patty—she was brainwashed. Brainwashing is, by definition, the "process of systematically, forcibly, and intensively indoctrinating a person to destroy or weaken his beliefs and ideas so that he becomes willing to accept different or opposite beliefs or ideas."[3] Often in brainwashing, as well as its just-as-questionable counterpart, deprogramming, various stresses are forced upon a person, including food and sleep deprivation and forcing them to watch images and hear propaganda that disagree with their beliefs. Patricia Hearst was confined to a closet for weeks, and repeatedly taught the beliefs that she finally accepted.

Living in a media-saturated world can be a similar experience. Images and words are constantly being thrust upon us that either deny the existence of God or subtly twist our idea of Him. What's more, many of the people around us do not know Jesus Christ, and do not live by His Word. They may subtly or openly try to convince us that Christianity is all a big hoax. If we continually soak in these messages, we will sooner or later transfer our loyalties from our Father to our "kidnappers," join their army, and shoot their guns.

## TRY IT OUT

1. Go on a TV fast. If you don't watch TV, fast from reading anything but the Bible for one week. During the week, study out a topic from the Word using the concordance. Spend the amount of time you would normally spend in the other activities.

2. Write an essay entitled, "Is There an Absolute Truth?" A good resource book is *Inside the Soul of a New Generation,* by Tim Celek and Dieter Zander.

3. This is for very brave people: Offer to teach an adult Sabbath school class one week.

4. This is for less brave people: Write a letter to yourself from God entitled, "Ten Things I Died to Tell You."

5. This is for all people: Think of a religious leader you admire and ask them if you can pick their brain for 15 minutes. Have a list of questions ready for them. You will be blessed, and they will be touched that you are interested. Toward the end of the talk, ask them if they have any questions for you.

# I Want It All

## CROSS-EXAMINE THE WITNESS

 *Our witness is Jason Williams from St. John's, Newfoundland, Canada. He plans to study theology, so how appropriate for him to talk about truth.*

QUESTION: JASON, WHY IS HONESTY IMPORTANT TO YOU?

Honesty is an important part of the Christian's life. In the Ten Commandments God specified that all people should "not bear false witness" against their neighbor (Exodus 20:16). In John 8:44 Jesus spoke of Satan and said that "he is a liar, and the father of it."

Certainly, if we are to be God's children, sons and daughters bought with the blood of Jesus at Calvary, we will want to be holy, pure, faithful, and honest in our daily lives. That is the way God wants us to be. But we must remember that we cannot be honest by ourselves. The way we attain to this honesty is to receive the Truth itself, Jesus Christ—the way, the truth, and the life. When we let Him in, He creates a new heart within us—a heart that is pure and honest. This, with the help of the Holy Spirit, gives us power to live by the example Jesus gave us.

One day we will see Him welcome us into the new earth, where we will receive the kingdom Jesus has gone to prepare. Honesty is the best way to live—the *only* way that we can live forever!

---

[1] Brian Avery, "The Symbionese Liberation Army," www.home.earthlink.net/~dwgsht/sla.html.

[2] *Ibid.*

[3] Discussion with David Bunds, www.fountain.btinternet.co.uk/koresh/bunds/html.